GROWING

YOUR

FAITH

GROWING
YOUR
FAITH

How to Mature in Christ

JERRY BRIDGES

BEST-SELLING AUTHOR OF *The Pursuit of Holiness*

NAVPRESS

Discipleship Inside Out™

© 2004 by Gerald D. Bridges

All rights reserved. No part of this publication may be reproduced in any form without written permission from NavPress, P.O. Box 35001, Colorado Springs, CO 80935. www.navpress.com

NAVPRESS and the NAVPRESS logo are registered trademarks of NavPress. Absence of ® in connection with marks of NavPress or other parties does not indicate an absence of registration of those marks.

ISBN 978-1-57683-475-6

Cover design by David Carlson Design
Cover image by Corbis
Creative Team: Don Simpson, Darla Hightower, Pat Reinheimer

This book adapted from previously published material.

Some of the anecdotal illustrations in this book are true to life and are included with the permission of the persons involved. All other illustrations are composites of real situations, and any resemblance to people living or dead is coincidental.

Unless otherwise identified, all Scripture quotations in this publication are taken from the HOLY BIBLE: NEW INTERNATIONAL VERSION® (NIV®). Copyright © 1973, 1978, 1984 by International Bible Society. Used by permission of Zondervan Publishing House. All rights reserved. Other versions used include: The Holy Bible, English Standard Version, (ESV) copyright © 2001 by Crossway Bibles, a division of Good News Publishers. Used by permission. All rights reserved; and the *Williams New Testament* (WMS) by Charles B. Williams, © 1937, 1965, 1966, by Edith S. Williams, Moody Bible Institute of Chicago.

Bridges, Jerry.
  Growing your faith : how to mature in Christ / Jerry Bridges.
    p. cm.
Includes bibliographical references.
  ISBN 1-57683-475-1
  1. Christian life. I. Title.
  BV4501.3.B752 2004
  248.4--dc22

                              2003014820

Printed in the United States of America

5 6 7 8 9 10 11 / 15 14 13 12 11

To

Dwight and Lucille Custis

and the congregation of

Trinity Bible Church

PREFACE

DURING THE FIRST three years of my Christian life, I grew very little. I didn't know how to grow my faith, and I didn't realize I should be intentional about it. I think this is true of many believers today, even some who have been Christians for several years. They are not growing because they don't know how to grow and are not even aware that they should be growing. This book aims to encourage believers, both new and old, to grow and to provide basic instruction for being intentional about it.

To borrow an expression from the collegiate world, I would describe this book as *Christian Growth 101*. It is meant to be basic instruction for spiritual growth. At the same time, I believe already-growing Christians will profit from a review of these principles of growth. We all need to be continually refreshed in the truths we have learned because we have a natural tendency to drift away from them. So to quote the apostle Peter, "I will . . . remind you of these things, even though you know them and are firmly established in the truth you now have" (2 Peter 1:12). Someone has said that we need to be reminded more than we need to be instructed. Therefore, I do not apologize for, so to speak, "re-plowing old ground."

Much of the material in this book has appeared in my earlier works. This is by design. The editorial team at NavPress thought I had addressed key principles of spiritual growth in previous writings, but that they were scattered among eight different books. In this book, I have gathered into one volume all I have written about Christian growth in those early works making it more accessible in a single book.

In the following section, *Acknowledgments,* I have listed the appropriate chapters from the various books from which each chapter is drawn. In every instance, the previous material has been heavily revised and adapted for this book. Anyone wishing to explore more fully what I have said on a given subject can easily locate the original material by referring to the *Acknowledgments* section.

There are four people who deserve a special word of thanks for their part in the preparation of this book. First: Don Simpson of NavPress, who not only served as primary editor but who also worked with me in selecting material from the earlier books to include in this volume. Second: Louise Bridgewater and Brenda Lagasse, who rendered invaluable service in typing and proofreading all the adaptations of the original material in a very short time frame. Finally: my wife Jane, who exercised considerable patience during the time I had to set aside activities we had planned to do together so that I could meet the tight deadline for this book. Thanks to each one of you.

ACKNOWLEDGMENTS

CHAPTER 1 IS new written material from spoken messages given at various times, none of which has previously appeared in print.

Chapter 2 is adapted from *Transforming Grace,* NavPress, 1991 (chapter 6, "Compelled by Love").

Chapter 3 is adapted from *The Discipline of Grace,* NavPress, 1994 (chapter 5, "Disciplined by Grace").

Chapter 4 is adapted from *The Discipline of Grace* (chapter 6, "Transformed into His Likeness").

Chapter 5 is all new material, although it draws upon a lifetime of teaching and writing on the importance of the Bible in Christian growth.

Chapter 6 is adapted from *The Discipline of Grace* (chapter 10, "The Discipline of Convictions"). Some new material not previously published has been added.

Chapter 7 is adapted from a small section of *Transforming Grace* (chapter 8, "Holiness: A Gift of God's Grace," page 115) and from *The Discipline of Grace* (chapter 8, "Dependent Discipline").

Chapter 8 is adapted from *The Crisis of Caring,* P&R Publishing

Company: Phillipsburg, N.J., 1992 (chapter 5, "Spiritual Fellowship"), used by permission.

Chapter 9 is adapted from *The Discipline of Grace* (chapter 6, "Transformed into His Likeness," pp. 105-109) and from *The Gospel for Real Life,* NavPress, 2002 (chapter 15, "The Gospel and Sanctification").

Chapter 10 is adapted from a small section of *The Pursuit of Holiness,* NavPress, 1978, 1996 (chapter 2, "The Holiness of God") and from *The Discipline of Grace* (chapter 11, "The Discipline of Choices").

Chapter 11 is adapted from *The Practice of Godliness,* NavPress, 1983, 1996 (chapter 1, "Value for All Things" and chapter 17, "Love") and from *Transforming Grace* (chapter 13, "Garments of Grace").

Chapter 12 is adapted from spoken messages given on the subject of trusting God and from *The Discipline of Grace* (chapter 13, "The Discipline of Adversity").

Chapter 13 is adapted from *The Crisis of Caring* (chapter 11, "The Fellowship of Serving"), used by permission.

Chapter 14 is adapted from *The Joy of Fearing God,* WaterBrook Press: Colorado Springs, Colo., 1997 (chapter 14, "He Is Worthy"), used by permission.

THE NECESSITY OF SPIRITUAL GROWTH

CHAPTER I

THE FOUNDATION FOR GROWTH

S OME YEARS AGO we planted a tree on the west side of our house expecting it to grow and eventually shade us from the afternoon sun. We were disappointed because, for some reason, the tree didn't grow. It didn't die, but neither did it grow. Possibly, it was because it was poor stock to begin with. After some effort to spur its growth, we finally had it removed and replaced with a tree that happily has grown. Soon this tree will be tall enough to fulfill the purpose for which it was planted. It will shade our house from the hot afternoon sun.

Growth is a normal expression of life. Whether we think of plants, animals, or people, we expect them to grow until they reach maturity. When something or someone doesn't grow, we know something is wrong.

Growth is also a normal expression of the Christian life. The New Testament writers assume growth and constantly urge us to pursue it. Peter urges us to "Grow in the grace and knowledge of our Lord and Savior Jesus Christ" (2 Peter 3:18). Paul instructs us that by "speaking the truth in love, we will in all things grow up into him who is the Head, that is, Christ" (Ephesians 4:15).

In fact, in distinction from the physical realm, Christians should never stop growing spiritually. Paul commended the Thessalonian believers for their seeking to please God and to love other believers. And yet, in both instances, he urged them to do so "more and more" (1 Thessalonians 4:1,10). He wanted them to continue to grow in these aspects of their Christian lives. There is no such thing as an "adult Christian" who no longer needs to grow. Growth is not only normal for new believers but also for those who have walked with God fifty years or more.

Of course, almost all growth (both physical and spiritual) is incremental. We can't watch either plants or people grow before our eyes. We can only observe it over time. This is also true in the Christian life. And, of course, different people grow at different rates. And none of us grow at the same steady rate all the time. But even when we allow for differences in people and different eras of growth in our individual lives, the fact remains that we should all be growing spiritually. When a believer doesn't grow, something is wrong!

This book assumes that those who read it want to grow. There are some people who for one reason or another don't seem to want to grow, and that's a different story. But if you have picked up this book, it is likely that you want to grow and that you are looking for all the help you can get. That's my attitude when I pick up a Christian book, and I assume it's also yours. So we need to address the question: How do we grow spiritually?

Let's think about physical growth for a moment. Children grow without thinking about it. In fact, our basic physical growth (height and body structure) is beyond our control. My older brother grew to be 6'2" tall. I expected to follow suit. So when I realized I had topped out at 5'9 1/2" (I always add the half inch), I was quite disappointed.

But there was nothing I could do. As much as I wanted to be at least 6' tall, I couldn't make myself grow.

However, we all know that intellectual growth or growth in a physical skill is a different matter. Once a little girl starts to school, she must apply herself if she is to grow intellectually. Later on, if she wants to play on the basketball team, she must again apply herself both mentally and physically.

Eventually, this little girl becomes a young woman and goes off to college. Now she wants to prepare herself for a professional career of some kind. She gives herself to her studies because she desires to excel in her chosen career field. Obviously, some students are more diligent than others. Some are content to simply muddle through and get a degree. But those who want to excel apply themselves. Intellectual or professional growth doesn't just happen. It only comes with intentional effort. And usually the degree of growth is directly related to the degree of effort.

The same is true in spiritual growth. It doesn't just happen. In fact, it doesn't even happen by spiritual osmosis, that is, by just being around other believers and unconsciously assimilating their spirituality. Spiritual growth occurs as a result of *intentional* and *appropriate* effort. The word *intentional* implies a diligent pursuit of a clear goal. *Appropriate* indicates that we must use the God-given ways of growth given to us in the Bible. We usually refer to these ways of growth as "spiritual disciplines." We'll explore what these disciplines are in later chapters. But for now, we must lay an important foundation—the foundation of grace.

Over 150 years ago Archibald Alexander, the first president of Princeton Theological Seminary, wrote some thoughts on "hindrances to spiritual growth." The first hindrance he listed was "a defect in our belief in the freeness of divine grace."[1] In his elaboration on that statement, he essentially said that a correct understanding of God's grace and a consistent appropriation of it must be the foundation of all our personal efforts to grow spiritually.

===

WHAT IS GRACE?

Because grace is foundational to our Christian growth, it's important that we have a correct understanding of it. Unfortunately, there is a lot of misunderstanding about the nature of grace.

Perhaps the most common misconception of grace is captured in a statement I once read: Grace is the idea that we are loved and accepted by God just as we are and that God's approval does not have to be earned; it is simply there. Here, God seems to be pictured as the proverbial, indulgent, divine grandfather in the sky who smiles down upon us regardless of our behavior and character. This seems to be typical of the average person's understanding of God's grace.

By contrast, however, the Bible teaches us that the grace of God "teaches us to say 'No' to ungodliness and worldly passions, and to live self-controlled, upright and godly lives" (Titus 2:12). God does love us and accepts us as sinners "just as we are." But He does not leave us that way. Rather, by the same grace through which He saves us, He sets about to change everyone who experiences that grace.

The statement that "God's approval does not have to be earned but is simply there" is not true. God's approval *does* have to be earned. But the gospel tells us that His approval was earned for us by Jesus Christ in His sinless life and sin-bearing death. It is true that God's favor does not have to be earned *by us*. In fact, it cannot be earned by us. But it comes to us without earning because Jesus paid for it in our place as our substitute.

MISCONCEPTION!

18

What about the time-honored definition of grace as *God's unmerited favor*? While it is not wrong, I believe it is inadequate. So here is a definition that I believe captures the biblical meaning of grace: *Grace is God's favor through Christ to people who deserve His disfavor.*

There are two elements in this definition that are missing in the shorter definition above. The first is the realization that we actually deserve God's disfavor because of our sin. Or to put it starkly, in biblical terms, we deserve His *curse* (see Galatians 3:10).

The second element that I have added is the term *through Christ*. It is through Christ, because of His death on the cross, that we don't receive the disfavor or curse we all deserve. As Paul wrote in Galatians 3:13, "Christ redeemed us from the curse of the law by becoming a curse for us." And it is through Christ, because of His perfect obedience to the whole will of God, that we receive the blessings we don't deserve. Christ bore our curse and earned our blessing. That is the meaning of grace.

We see this concept of Christ bearing our curse and earning our blessing set forth in 2 Corinthians 5:21: "God made him who had no sin to be sin for us, so that in him we might become the righteousness of God."

In this somewhat difficult-to-understand language, Paul was saying that God charged our sin to Christ and credited His righteousness to us. Or to paraphrase: "God treated Christ as we deserved to be treated in order that He might treat us as He deserved to be treated." That is grace.

So grace is God's favor to us through Christ, but God's favor is much more than simply a favorable disposition toward us. God's grace is always presented in Scripture as God in action toward us for our good. For example, God's grace saves us (see Ephesians 2:8-9; Romans 5:1); it gives us spiritual strength (see 2 Timothy 2:1); sustains us in times of trial (see 2 Corinthians 12:9); and equips us for ministry (see Romans 12:6). We can say that every blessing that comes to us is an expression of God's grace. That means that Christ *earned* all those blessings for us by His sinless life and sin-bearing death. – GRASP!

It is important that we grasp this cardinal truth before we proceed to the various means of growth God has given us. Otherwise, we will subtly and unconsciously begin to see these disciplines that God has given us for our good as disciplines to be practiced in order to earn or maintain His favor. *DON'T LET*

Remember our definition of grace. Jesus has already earned God's favor for you. Just as you can do nothing to earn your salvation (the most important blessing of all), so you can do nothing to earn God's favor in your daily life. If you do not grasp this truth, the spiritual disciplines that are intended to help you grow will become burdensome duties you think you must practice in order to maintain God's favor. *OR THIS!*

———

THE BOOKENDS

Let's look at this truth another way. Have you ever tried to arrange some books on a shelf without first setting up bookends? You know what happens. The books begin to fall, first sidewise, and then one or more of them inevitably tumbles to the floor. In frustration, you finally do what you should have done at the beginning. You get some bookends and put them in place.

Now, as we consider the various means by which Christians grow, think of each one of them as a book you are putting on the shelf of your life. In order to keep those books in place, you need two bookends.

The first bookend we need to set in place is *the righteousness of Christ*. The most important question any person can ask is: How can I, a sinful person, be accepted by an infinitely holy and righteous God?

Paul tells us that it is by trusting in the righteousness of Christ. Paul himself was a devout Jew, and his religious credentials were impressive during the time in which he lived (see Philippians 3:4-6). And yet Paul said he counted all his religious credentials as rubbish in order that he might "gain Christ and be found in him, not having a righteousness of my own that comes from the law [that is, by trying to earn God's acceptance through my own obedience to God's law], but that which is through faith in Christ—the righteousness that comes from God and is by faith" (Philippians 3:8-9).

Paul found his acceptance with God not in his own imperfect obedience, as impressive as it was, but by trusting in the perfect righteousness of Jesus Christ which God credits to all who trust in Him as Savior. This is what faith is—trusting in Jesus Christ alone as one's Savior.

In Romans 3 and 4 and Galatians 2, Paul uses a legal term to describe this righteousness that he and all believers have in Christ. It is the word *justification*, which comes from the verb "to justify" and which means to declare righteous. In other words, when we trust in Christ as our Savior, God justifies us or declares us righteous on the basis that He has charged our sin to Christ and credited His righteousness to us. God does this at the very moment we trust in Christ. So we can say that justification is a point-in-time event that happened in our past. But for Paul, justification was more than a past event. It seems obvious from a close reading of Philippians 3:9 that he also considered it a *present reality*. Every day Paul lived in the glorious reality that he stood before God clothed in the righteousness of Christ and accepted by Him on the basis of that righteousness.

If you and I are to succeed in putting on the shelf of our lives the various volumes of Christian disciplines that we need in order to grow, we absolutely must have the bookend of Christ's righteousness firmly in place.

The second bookend we must set in place is *the power of Christ.* Just as our acceptance with God must come through the righteousness of Christ, so our power to live the Christian life must come from Christ as well. Too often we try to grow by our own willpower and self-discipline. We assume that if we read the Bible enough and pray enough, we will grow. We approach the Christian life much like a student approaches a difficult course in college—just buckle down and try harder. That attitude assumes that we have the ability within ourselves to grow into maturity as believers. But as Jesus indicated in John 15:5, we have no ability within ourselves to grow. All of the ability must come from Him.

GOOD EXAMPLE!

Think of an electronic appliance that you use either for personal care or in the kitchen. I think of my electric shaver. That shaver has within its case a small motor that causes the shaver to do its job. But that motor has no power of its own. It is completely dependent on an external source of electric current. Without the supply of that power, it is useless.

Heart of flesh, not a heart of stone!

You and I have been given a new heart at the time of our conversion (see Ezekiel 36:26-27). A fundamental change has indeed taken place in our inner being. We really are new creations in Christ. To *←2 cor.* stay with the shaver analogy, we now have a new motor designed to receive the electric current. But the power is still outside of us. It resides in Jesus Christ and is applied to our hearts by the Holy Spirit as we depend on Him.

This is why Paul makes such statements as "I can do everything through him who gives me strength" (Philippians 4:13) and "To this end [that is, pursuing his ministry] I labor, struggling with all his energy, which so powerfully works in me" (Colossians 1:29).

Paul expected to grow in his own spiritual life, and he expected to be fruitful in his ministry. His confidence, however, was not based on his own ability or determination but in the fact that he could rely on

Confidence of CHRIST

the power of Christ working in him to enable him.

We will explore in more detail in chapter 7 how we draw upon the power of Christ. For now, we just want to become aware that we need these two "bookends."

One further observation will be helpful, however. Bookends usually come in pairs, both with a common design. Our spiritual bookends of Christian growth also come as a pair. The common element of their design is the word *dependence.* We are dependent upon the righteousness of Christ for our acceptance with God, and we are dependent on the power of Christ for our ability to pursue spiritual growth.

This idea of dependence is totally contrary to our cultural way of thinking. We want to earn our acceptance with God by our own performance. We've been taught in any number of ways that "there is no such thing as a free lunch" and "you get what you pay for." The idea of basing our standing with God on someone else's payment—on the sinless life and sin-bearing death of Christ—is hard for us to accept.

Similarly, we've been taught to be self-reliant—to reach down deep within ourselves to find whatever strength we need. We've been assured that we can do anything if we just believe in ourselves and try hard enough. The idea of looking outside of ourselves for the power to grow spiritually runs counter to all we've been taught, and it's also difficult to accept.

But if we are going to experience any success at all in putting on the shelf of our lives the various "books" of Christian growth, we must first set in place these two bookends. We must learn to depend on both the righteousness of Christ and the power of Christ. This is what it means to live by grace. And this is why grace is foundational to spiritual growth.

My Life Application

SO TRUE!

CHAPTER 2

COMPELLED BY LOVE

L IVING BY GRACE means you are free from having to earn God's blessings by your obedience or practice of spiritual disciplines. If you have trusted in Christ as your Savior, you are loved and accepted by God through the merit of Jesus, and you are blessed by God through the merit of Jesus. Nothing you ever do will cause Him to love you any more or any less. He loves you strictly by His grace given to you through Jesus.[1]

SO TRUE!

How does this emphasis on God's free and sovereign grace make you feel? Does it make you a little nervous? Does it seem a bit scary to hear that nothing you do will ever make God love you any more or bless you any more? Do you think, *Well, if you take the pressure off like that and tell me all of my effort will never earn me one blessing, then I'm afraid I'll slack off and stop doing the things I need to do to live a disciplined Christian life?*

This type of response is always a possibility. In fact, if our concept of grace does not expose us to that possible misunderstanding, then we do not thoroughly understand grace. I believe it is because we are afraid of this attitude that we often change the doctrine of grace into a doctrine of works.

SO TRUE!

The apostle Paul recognized that God's grace can be misunderstood when he wrote, "Shall we go on sinning so that grace may increase?" (Romans 6:1). The late Dr. Martyn Lloyd-Jones of England, one of the ablest and most respected Bible expositors of the twentieth century, said this in response to that question:

> The true preaching of the gospel of salvation by grace alone always leads to the possibility of this charge being brought against it. There is no better test as to whether a man is really preaching the New Testament gospel of salvation than this, that some people might misunderstand it and misinterpret it to mean that it really amounts to this, that because you are saved by grace alone it does not matter at all what you do; you can go on sinning as much as you like because it will redound all the more to the glory of grace.[2]

The grace of salvation is the same grace by which we live the Christian life. We are not saved by grace and blessed by works. Paul said in Romans 5:2, "We have gained access by faith into *this grace in which we now stand*" (emphasis added). We are not only justified by grace through faith, we *stand* every day in this same grace. And just as the preaching of salvation by grace is open to misunderstanding, so is the teaching of living by grace.

The solution to the problem of misunderstanding and abusing God's grace is not to add works to grace. Rather, the solution is to be so gripped by the magnificence and boundless generosity of God's grace that we respond out of gratitude rather than out of a sense of duty. As Stephen Brown said, "The problem [isn't] that we made the gospel too good. The problem is that we didn't make it good enough."[3]

NOT THE SOLUTION!

26

Too often when we think of Christian growth, we load down the gospel of the grace of God with a lot of "oughts." "If I'm going to grow, I ought to do this," and "I ought to do that." "I ought to be more committed, more disciplined, more obedient." When we think or teach this way, we are in danger of substituting duty and obligation for a loving response to God's grace.

WE OFTEN DO THIS. [handwritten margin note]

Let me be very clear at this point. We should seek to practice commitment, discipline, and obedience. We should be thoroughly committed to submission to the lordship of Jesus Christ in every area of life. But we should be committed in these areas out of a grateful response to God's grace, not to try to earn God's blessings. ← *It's already done!* [handwritten margin note]

Our *motivation* for commitment, discipline, and obedience is important to God, perhaps even more so, than our *performance.* As Ernest F. Kevan wrote, "The Law's demands are inward, touching motive and desire, and are not concerned solely with outward action."[4]

David said to Solomon, "And you, my son Solomon, acknowledge the God of your father, and serve him with wholehearted devotion and with a willing mind, for the LORD searches every heart and understands every motive behind the thoughts" (1 Chronicles 28:9). The apostle Paul echoed the importance of motives when he wrote that, at the Lord's coming, "He . . . will expose the motives of men's hearts" (1 Corinthians 4:5).

He is THAT personal! [handwritten margin note]

← God searches the heart and understands every motive. To be acceptable to Him, our motives must spring from a love for Him and a desire to glorify Him. Our efforts to grow performed from a legalistic motive—that is, a fear of the consequences or to gain favor with God—are not pleasing to God. Thus, our desire to grow and to please God is not truly good unless it is motivated by a love for God and a desire to glorify Him. But we cannot have such a God-ward motivation if we think we must earn God's favor by our disciplines, or if we fear we may forfeit God's favor by our lack of them. Such a works-oriented motivation is essentially self-serving; it is prompted more by what we think we can gain or lose from God than by a grateful response to the grace He has already given us through Jesus Christ.

Living under the grace of God instead of under a sense of duty frees us from such a self-serving motivation. It frees us to obey God and serve Him as a loving and thankful response to Him for our salvation and for blessings already guaranteed us by His grace. Consequently, a heartfelt grasp of God's grace — far from creating an indifferent or careless attitude in us — will actually provide us the only motivation that is pleasing to Him. Only when we are thoroughly convinced that the Christian life is entirely of grace will we be able joyfully to practice the disciplines that help us grow.

Let me clarify one thing further, lest I be misunderstood. When I stress a God-ward motivation for our discipline and obedience, I am not talking about inclination or feeling. We are not to wait until we "feel like" having a quiet time to have one. And we certainly are not to wait until we are so inclined to obey God's commands. Motive has nothing to do with feelings or inclination; rather, it refers to the *reason* why we do, or don't do, something. For the person living by grace, that reason should be a loving response to the abundant grace of God already manifested in Christ.

PAY CLOSE ATTENTION.

═══════

COMPELLED BY LOVE

In 2 Corinthians 5:14-15, Paul said,

> For Christ's love compels us, because we are con-
> vinced that one died for all, and therefore all died.
> And he died for all, that those who live should no

28

longer live for themselves but for him who died for
them and was raised again.

While there is a lot of spiritual truth in this passage, the essential
teaching is that Christ's love compels us to live no longer for ourselves
but for Him who died for us and was raised again. The idea here is
commitment to the lordship of Jesus Christ in every area of our lives.
We are to live no longer for ourselves but for Him. We are to make His
will the rule of our lives and His glory the goal for which we live. This
is what spiritual growth is all about. But what is the wellspring of this
commitment? What motivating principle will cause a person to live no
longer for himself but for God?

Paul said the love of Christ compels us to make this kind of
commitment and to carry it out day by day. *Compel* is a strong word
and often has a negative association with force or coercion. But here
its meaning is positive. Charles Hodge wrote that the love of Christ
"coerces, or presses, and therefore impels. It is the governing influence
which controls the life."[5] It is not a fear of consequences or expecta-
tion of reward that motivates Paul. Rather, the love of Christ manifested in dying for him is the driving force of his life. ←—this should be my motivation.

The Williams New Testament is well regarded for its careful rendering of the tenses of the Greek verbs, and it is particularly helpful
here. Williams translated the first phrase of 2 Corinthians 5:14 in this
manner: "For the love of Christ continuously constrains me." Note the
use of the word *continuously,* indicating that Christ's love is the constant wellspring of Paul's motivation every day. Paul never lost sight
of, never forgot, never took for granted the death of Christ for him.
And as he reflected on this infinite love manifested in Christ's death,
he was motivated, no, he was compelled and impelled to live for the
One who died for him and rose again.

Sometimes when I talk about living by grace instead of by works, people get nervous. Some have warned me against "going too far" by telling me stories of people who, after hearing a message on God's grace, have committed some grossly sinful act. I grant the possibility that grace can be so misunderstood. But I believe that, in most instances where people apparently abuse grace, they have not truly understood grace as I defined it in chapter 1. Rather, they have understood it in the popular idea that grace means God doesn't care how we live.

People who truly understand the grace of God, not just intellectually but in the very core of their being, will not abuse grace by living irresponsibly. Once while reading through Romans in my daily Bible reading, I came to Romans 4 and read these words in verses 7 and 8:

"Blessed are they whose transgressions are forgiven, whose sins are covered. Blessed is the man whose sin the Lord will never count against him."

When I read, "Blessed is the man whose sin the Lord will *never* count against him" (emphasis added), I wept with joy and gratitude. What a fantastic encouragement that God will *never* judge me for *any* of my sins. I know I have as wicked a sinful nature as anyone else, and apart from the influence of the Holy Spirit in my life, I am fully capable of the so-called gross sins of immorality, drunkenness, stealing, and the like. But those are not the sins that trouble me at this time. Rather, I struggle with what I call "refined" sins: selfishness, pride, impatience, a critical attitude, and a judgmental spirit.

Despite my calling those areas "refined" sins, they are nevertheless very real sins. They are sins for which I would not want to give account at the judgment bar of God. They are sins that, apart from the atoning death of Christ for me, would send me to eternal hell. And, if God operated on the basis of merit instead of grace in this life, they are sins that would forfeit all blessing from Him. In short those "refined" sins are very troublesome.

So when I read that God will never count against me my selfishness, my pride, my impatience, and so on, I wept for joy. I stopped reading and uttered a prayer of deep, heartfelt thanksgiving to God for His gracious forgiveness. Then what did I do? Did I say to myself, *Well, if God is not going to count these sins against me, it really doesn't matter whether or not I deal with them?* Did I think, *Since God is not going to count them against me anyway, I might as well not bother with all the spiritual pain of putting to death those ungodly traits?*

Of course I did not think like that. Instead I asked God to purge those sinful traits from my character. I asked Him to enable me to become more and more aware of specific instances when I was committing those sins so that I could, by His Spirit, put them to death as Paul tells us to do in Romans 8:13. I was compelled by His love to seek to put away those sins.

REVERENCE FOR GOD

Along with a sense of profound gratitude to God for His grace, we should be motivated to grow and obey God by a deep sense of reverence for Him. When Joseph was tempted to immorality by Potiphar's wife, his response was, "How then could I do such a wicked thing and sin against God?" (Genesis 39:9). He did not calculate the possible wrath of Potiphar or the forfeiture of God's blessing. He was motivated by reverence for God. He was concerned about disobedience to a sovereign, holy God, even though that God had allowed him to be sold into slavery by his own brothers.

The apostle Paul combined these two elements of a God-ward

motivation—gratitude and reverence—when he wrote to the Corinthian believers, "Since we have these promises, dear friends, let us purify ourselves from everything that contaminates body and spirit, perfecting holiness out of reverence for God" (2 Corinthians 7:1).

Paul referred to the promises that God would be our God and Father and would make us His sons and daughters. Philip Hughes commented on this passage, "The logical consequence of possessing such promises is that Christ's followers should make a complete break with every form of unhealthy compromise."[6] Here again we see that promises come before duty and that duty flows out of a heartfelt response to the promises of God.

But Paul went on to say, "out of reverence for God." *Reverence* is a sense of profound awe, respect, and devotion. It is a recognition of God's intrinsic worthiness, the infinite majesty of His being, and the infinite perfection of His character. Because of who He is and what He is, God is infinitely worthy of my most diligent and loving obedience, even if I never receive a single blessing from His hand. The fact is, of course, I have received innumerable blessings from Him. But His worthiness is intrinsic within Himself; it is not conditioned on the number of blessings you or I receive from Him.

In Romans 12:1, Paul urges us, in view of God's mercy, to offer our bodies as living sacrifices to Him. Is He worthy of such sacrifice? Of course He is! He is infinitely worthy. But our motivation to obey and serve God cannot rise to such heights until we learn to live daily by grace and to experience freedom each day from the bondage of the performance treadmill.

I believe a genuine heart response to the worthiness of God is the highest possible motivation for pursuing the disciplines of spiritual growth and for obedience and service to God. But we cannot "break through" to that level of motivation until we are first motivated by His grace, mercy, and love. We cannot be free to think about God's worthiness and God's glory as long as we are struggling to earn our own acceptance with Him.

It's already done!

———

GROWING IN GRACE

The term *growing in grace* is most often used to indicate growth in Christian character. While I think that usage has merit, a more accurate meaning is continually to grow in our understanding of God's grace, especially as it applies to us personally, to become progressively more aware of our own continued spiritual bankruptcy and the unmerited, unearned, and undeserved favor of God. May we all grow in grace in this sense.

As we grow in grace this way, we will grow in our motivation to obey God out of a sense of gratitude and reverence to Him. Our obedience will always be imperfect in performance in this life. We will never perfectly obey Him until we are made perfect by Him. In the same way, our motives will never be consistently pure; there will frequently be some "merit points" mentality mixed in with our genuine love and reverence for God.

So don't be discouraged if you realize your motives have been largely merit-oriented. Just begin now to move toward grace motives. Begin to think daily about the implications of the grace of God in your life. Memorize and meditate frequently on such Scripture passages as Romans 12:1 and 2 Corinthians 5:14-15. Pray about the aspects of truth in those passages and ask God to motivate you by His mercy and love. When you recognize merit-oriented motives at work in you, renounce them and cast yourself completely on the grace of God and the merit of Jesus Christ. As you grow in grace in this way, you will indeed discover that His love compels you to live, not for yourself, but for Him who died for you and was raised again.

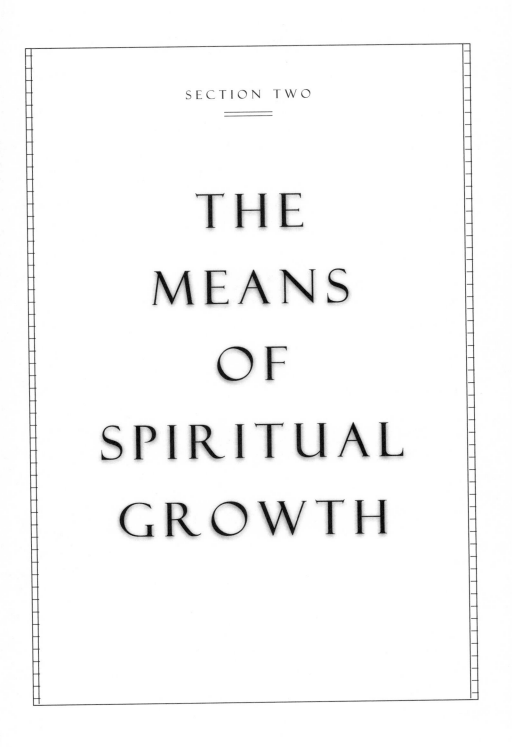

SECTION TWO

THE
MEANS
OF
SPIRITUAL
GROWTH

CHAPTER 3

DISCIPLINED BY GRACE

THE TITLE OF this chapter may seem like an oxymoron. Discipline may suggest restraint and legalism, rules and regulations, and a God who frowns on anyone who has fun. Grace, on the other hand, seems to mean freedom from any rules, spontaneous and unstructured living, and most of all a God who loves us unconditionally regardless of our sinful behavior.

MISUNDERSTANDING!

But such thinking reflects a misunderstanding of both grace and discipline. Consider, for example, Titus 2:11-12: "For the grace of God that brings salvation has appeared to all men. It teaches us to say 'No' to ungodliness and worldly passions, and to live self-controlled, upright and godly lives in this present age." As we can see from this passage, the same grace that brings salvation to us also disciplines us as believers. I referred briefly to this verse in chapter 1, but now we need to look at it more in depth if we are to understand the relationship between God's grace and our practice of spiritual disciplines. The verses actually read, "the grace of God . . . *teaches* us." The word translated as "teach," however, means much more than the usual idea we assign to it of imparting knowledge. Originally it was used as a term or the rearing of children and included not only instruction, but also admonition, reproof, and punishment, all administered in love and for the benefit of the child. The apostle Paul used the same word in Ephesians 6:4 when he charged fathers to bring up their children in the training (that is, discipline) and instruction of the Lord.

Used in a spiritual sense, discipline includes all instruction, all reproof and correction, and all providentially directed circumstances in our lives that are aimed at cultivating spiritual growth and godly character. And though in the physical realm children eventually reach adulthood and are no longer under the discipline of their parents, in the spiritual realm we remain under God's parental discipline as long as we live.

So we see that the very same grace that brings salvation also trains us to live lives that are pleasing to God. All of God's disciplinary processes are grounded in His grace—His unmerited and unconditional favor toward us. We tend to equate discipline with rules and performance standards; God equates it with firm but loving care for our souls.

When I was first introduced to the idea of Christian discipleship, I was given a list of seven spiritual disciplines I should practice every day—things such as a daily quiet time, Bible study, Scripture memorization, and prayer. All of those disciplines were very helpful to me, and I am grateful for every one of them. They gave me a structure for my spiritual growth. Indeed, we will examine some of these disciplines in later chapters.

However, while learning those disciplines I came to believe that my day-to-day relationship with God depended on how faithfully I performed them. No one actually told me that God's approval of me was based on my performance. Still, I developed a vague but real impression that God's smile or frown depended on whether or not I did my spiritual exercises. The challenge to be faithful in my quiet time, while good in itself, probably contributed to this impression.

My experience is not unusual. A friend of mine who ministers on a university campus told of a student who was exceptionally diligent in having his daily quiet time. My friend asked the student why he was so rigid in his practice, and the young man responded, "So nothing bad will happen to me." He was not being disciplined by grace but by fear.

We are performance-oriented by nature, and our culture, and sometimes our upbringing, reinforces this mindset. All too often a child's acceptance by his or her parents is based on the child's performance, and this certainly tends to be true in our society. We carry this same type of thinking into our relationship with God. So, whether it is our response to God's discipline of us or our practice of those spiritual disciplines that are so good and helpful, we tend to think it is the "law" of God rather than the grace of God that disciplines us.

[handwritten margin note: SO TRUE! I DO THIS TOO!]

Paul said, though, that it is the very same grace, God's unmerited favor, that brought salvation to us in the first place—that disciplines us. This means that all our responses to God's dealings with us and all our practice of the spiritual disciplines must be based on the knowledge that God is dealing with us in grace. And it means that all our effort to teach godly living and spiritual maturity to others must be grounded in grace. If we fail to teach that discipline is by grace, people will assume, as I did, that it is by performance.

That is why we must continue to emphasize the "bookends" of Christian growth, which I wrote about in chapter 1. Once we begin to grow we have just as difficult a time believing that God relates to us every day on the basis of grace as a person has believing that God saves by grace instead of by works. So we must continue to come back to God's grace every day. And we must continue to teach it and preach it to those whom we may be discipling in some way, whether in a Sunday school class or Bible study we are teaching or in a one-to-one mentoring relationship. Spiritual growth must be based on God's grace.

SALVATION AND DISCIPLINE ARE INSEPARABLE

Another truth we see in Titus 2:11-12 is that salvation and spiritual discipline are inseparable. The grace that brings salvation to us also disciplines us. It does not do the one without the other. That is, God never saves people and leaves them alone to continue in their immaturity and sinful lifestyle. Those whom He saves, He disciplines. Paul said this thought another way in Philippians 1:6: "He who began a good work in you will carry it on to completion until the day of Christ Jesus."

This thought is both encouraging and sobering. It is encouraging because it assures us that our spiritual growth is not left to our initiative, nor is it dependent upon our wisdom to know in which areas and in which direction we need to grow. Rather, it is God Himself who initiates and superintends our spiritual growth. This is not to say that we have no responsibility to respond to God's spiritual child-training in our lives, but it is to say that He is the one in charge of our training.

Of course, God will use others, such as our pastors and other mature Christians, as His agents, and He will use various means, primarily His Word and circumstances, to discipline us, but He is the one who takes the ultimate responsibility. And as the one who is infinite in wisdom, He knows exactly which means to use in our lives at any given time. Our response then should be to trust Him and obey Him, and, to use words from the writer of Hebrews, to pray that He will "work in us what is pleasing to him" (13:21).

At the same time this inseparability of God's grace and spiritual discipline is a sobering truth. One has only to look around at Christendom, particularly in the United States, to see that there is a vast multitude of people who claim to have trusted in Christ at some time but do not seem to have experienced any of the discipline of grace. They may have walked an aisle, signed a card, or even prayed a prayer, but grace is not teaching them to say no to ungodliness and worldly passions, let alone to live self-controlled, upright, and godly lives. Essentially, their lives are no different today than they were before they professed to have trusted Christ. *[margin note: SAD REALITY PRAY FOR THEM!]*

As I think of these people, I am reminded of the words of Hebrews 12:8, "If you are not disciplined (and everyone undergoes discipline), then you are illegitimate children and not true sons." And Jesus Himself said, "Not everyone who says to me, 'Lord, Lord,' will enter the kingdom of heaven, but only he who does the will of my Father who is in heaven" (Matthew 7:21). It is not those who have merely made a profession, but those in whose lives there is evidence of God's fatherly child-training who are the inheritors of eternal life.

This sobering truth should be reflected upon by each of us. Is God's grace disciplining me? The apostle Paul said, "Examine yourselves to see whether you are in the faith; test yourselves. Do you not realize that Christ Jesus is in you—unless, of course, you fail the test?" (2 Corinthians 13:5). And the apostle Peter exhorted us to "be all the more eager to make [our] calling and election sure" (2 Peter 1:10). Are you truly trusting in Jesus Christ alone as your Savior without mentally adding something of your own goodness? Is there any evidence that you have died to the reign of sin through union with Jesus Christ (see chapter 9)? And is the grace of God at work in you to discipline or train you so that you are growing spiritually? If your honest answer is "no," I urge you to come to Him believing His words that "whoever comes to me I will never drive away" (John 6:37). *[margin note: GREAT QUESTIONS TO ASK!]*

Let me be clear at this point. We do not pursue spiritual growth or the evidences of God's discipline to attain salvation. That would be salvation by works. Rather, God's discipline in our lives and the desire to grow on our part, be it ever so faint, is the inevitable result of receiving

God's gift of salvation by faith. As Martin Luther is so often quoted as saying, "We are saved by faith alone, but the faith that saves is never alone."

———

GRACE TEACHES US TO SAY NO

Still another truth we see in Titus 2:11-12 is that the discipline that grace administers to us has both a negative and a positive aspect. This should not surprise us when we think of discipline as child-training. Every responsible parent not only wants to deal with misbehavior in a child but also desires to promote positive character traits. Both are necessary in physical child-training, and both are necessary in the spiritual realm.

Grace first teaches us to say no to ungodliness and worldly passions. Ungodliness is usually equated with wickedness: that which is immoral, dishonest, cruel, evil, or debased (see, for example, Romans 1:18-32). Ungodliness, however, in its broadest form basically means disregarding God, ignoring Him, or not taking Him into account in one's life. It is a lack of fear and reverence for Him. The wickedness portrayed by Paul in Romans 1:18-32 all starts with ungodliness, with the idea that "although they knew God, they neither glorified him as God nor gave thanks to him" (verse 21). In this wider sense, then, a person may be highly moral and even benevolent and still be ungodly.

In a review of a book titled *Timelines of the Ancient World*, published by the Smithsonian Institution, the reviewer pointed out that even though great figures of history such as Alexander the Great are duly mentioned, not one word is said about the great men of the Bible such as Moses, Abraham, or David. Most revealing of all is the fact that not so much as a passing reference is made to Jesus Christ, despite the fact that the book uses the B.C. and A.D. suffixes in its dating. The editors unwittingly testified to the historical reality of Him around whom time is measured without even mentioning His name. I suspect the Smithsonian editors are nice, decent people—the kind you would enjoy having as your neighbor. But if their book is an indicator, they are ungodly people. They have no regard for God.

When we trust in Christ as our Savior, we bring a *habit* of ungodliness into our new life in Christ. Like the Smithsonian editors, we were accustomed to living without regard for God. As unbelievers, we cared neither for His glory nor His will. Basically, we ignored Him. But now that we have been delivered from the dominion of sin and brought under the reign of grace, grace teaches us to renounce this attitude (as well as actions) of ungodliness. Obviously this training does not occur all at once. In fact, God will be rooting out ungodliness from our lives as long as we live on this earth.

Grace also teaches us to say no to worldly passions, the inordinate desire for and preoccupation with the things of this life, such as possessions, prestige, pleasure, or power. Worldly passion is the opposite of the attitude Paul urged on us when he wrote, "Those who use the things of the world, [should live] as if not engrossed in them. For this world in its present form is passing away" (1 Corinthians 7:31).

What does it mean to say no to ungodliness and worldly passions? Basically it means a decisive break with those attitudes and practices. In one sense this decisive break is a divine act that occurred when we died to the dominion of sin in our lives. In fact, the tense of the Greek denotes the thought of *having denied* ungodliness and worldly passions, a prior act. In another sense, however, we are to work out this breach with sin by putting to death the misdeeds of the body (Romans 8:13). We will develop this idea further in chapter 10. But for now, to say no to worldly passions means "to abstain from sinful desires, which war against your soul" (1 Peter 2:11). It means that we recognize these desires as "deceitful" (Ephesians 4:22) and "evil" (James 1:14), and thus refuse the pleasure they suggest and the acts to which they beckon us.

The "OTHER"

═══════

GRACE TEACHES US TO SAY YES

Sometimes we can get the impression that the Christian life consists mainly of a series of negative prohibitions: "Do not do this" and "Do not do that." Prohibitions are definitely an important part of our spiritual discipline as attested by the fact that eight of the Ten Commandments are prohibitions (Exodus 20:1-19). We need the prohibitions that are set forth, not just in the Ten Commandments, but in all the life-application sections of the New Testament. Indwelling sin that remains in us has a persistent inclination toward worldly passions and needs the constant restraint of being denied its gratification.

The Christian life, however, should also be directed toward the positive expressions of Christian character, what Paul called the fruit of the Spirit in Galatians 5:22. In fact, all of Paul's ethical teaching is characterized by this twofold approach of putting off the old self and putting on the new self. For example, in Ephesians 4:22-24 he wrote, "You were taught, with regard to your former way of life, to put off your old self, which is being corrupted by its deceitful desires; to be made new in the attitude of your minds; and to put on the new self, created to be like God in true righteousness and holiness."

I like to think of this twofold approach of "putting off" and "putting on" as represented by the two blades of a pair of scissors. We readily recognize that a single scissors blade is useless as far as doing the job for which it was designed. The two blades must be joined together at the pivot point and must work in conjunction with each other to be effective. The scissors illustrates a spiritual principle: We must work simultaneously at putting off the characteristics of our old selves and putting on the characteristics of the new selves. One without the other is not effective.

Some believers seem to focus on putting off sinful practices but give little attention to what they are to put on. Too often the lives of such people become hard and brittle and probably self-righteous, since they tend to equate godliness with a defined list of "don'ts." Other believers tend to focus on putting on certain positive traits such as love, compassion, and kindness. But if they do not pay attention to the "don'ts" of Scripture, they can become careless in morality and ethics. So we need the dual focus of "putting off" and "putting on," and each should receive equal attention from us. We'll develop this more in later chapters, but for now I want us to see that spiritual growth does involve this twofold change in our character.

PAY CLOSE ATTENTION.

In the Titus passage we are considering, the positive aspect of the Christian life is expressed by the phrase, "[It teaches us] to live self-controlled, upright and godly lives in this present age." These three words—self-controlled, upright, and godly—are considered by most Bible commentators to refer to actions with regard to one's self, one's neighbor, and to God. Self-control expresses the self-restraint we need to practice toward the good and legitimate things of life, as well as the outright denial of things clearly sinful. Upright or righteous conduct refers to just and right actions toward other people, doing to them what we would have them do to us (see Matthew 7:12). Godliness is having a regard for God's glory and God's will in every aspect of our lives, doing everything out of reverence and love for Him.

THE GOLDEN RULE

PRACTICAL CHRISTIAN LIVING

The apostle Paul summed up our three-directional duties of the Christian life in three words: self-controlled, upright, and godly. The context of his moral description of God's saving grace, however, is a whole series of moral exhortations from Titus 2:1 through 3:2. The instructions are addressed to the practical spiritual needs of various groups—older men, older women, young women, young men, slaves, Titus himself, and finally to all believers. From these specific instructions we can begin to "flesh out" what he means by self-controlled, upright, and godly lives.

This section of Scripture contains so many concise instructions that to elaborate on it would entail basically restating the passage. I urge you to prayerfully read it over yourself, asking God to help you evaluate your own life in light of Paul's instructions in practical Christian living. Don't just pay attention to the section that applies most to you (older men, older women, younger women, etc.). There are Christian virtues in each section that apply to all of us, regardless of age or gender.

I do call your attention to the three instances where Paul emphasized the importance of our Christian testimony before unbelievers. In Titus 2:5, he said, "so that no one will malign the word of God." In verse 8 he wrote, "so that those who oppose you may be ashamed because they have nothing bad to say about us." And then in his instructions to slaves, Paul concluded with, "so that in every way they will make the teaching about God our Savior attractive" (verse 10).

Paul was obviously concerned about the witness by life of the believers in Crete. In Romans he had said to the Jews, "God's name is blasphemed among the Gentiles because of you" (2:24), and he must have had a similar concern about the Cretan Christians. What would he say about us today? As the unbelieving world becomes increasingly hostile to true Christianity, it will be even more eager to find inconsistencies in our lives so it can ridicule God and His Word.

More than four hundred years ago the great reformer John Calvin voiced a similar concern when he wrote,

> Everything bad they [the ungodly] can seize hold of in our life is twisted maliciously against Christ and His teaching. The result is that by our fault God's sacred name is exposed to insult. The more closely we see ourselves being watched by our enemies, the more intent we should be to avoid their slanders, so that their ill-will strengthens us in the desire to do well.[1]

Therefore, as believers, we should seek to be exemplary in every aspect of our lives, doing our best for the sake of Christ and His gospel. Our work, our play, our driving, our shopping should all be done with a view that not only will unbelievers have nothing bad to say, but on the contrary, they will be attracted to the gospel they see at work in our lives.

―――

GRACE TEACHES US

With all this emphasis on practical Christian living, however, we must not lose sight of the fact that it is grace—not law—that teaches us. When I first became a Christian, I regarded the Bible largely as a rule book. My perception was that the Bible would tell me what to do (or not do), and I would simply obey. It was as easy as that, so I thought in my new Christian naiveté.

To me, then, the practical precepts of the Bible were no more than a statement of the law of God. They commanded but gave no ability to obey. Furthermore, they condemned me for my failure to obey them as I knew I ought. It seemed the more I tried, the more I failed.

I knew nothing of God's grace in enabling me to live the Christian life. I thought it was all by sheer grit and willpower. And just as importantly, I understood little of His forgiving grace through the blood of Christ. So I felt both guilty and helpless—guilty because of recurring sin patterns in my life and helpless to do anything about them.

My experience, however, was not unusual. In fact, I would say it is fairly typical, not just among new believers, but among many who have been Christians for years. That is why we need to understand that it is grace—not law—that disciplines us. Of course, Paul personified grace in the Titus passage. It is actually God in His grace, or by His grace, who disciplines us. Or to put it more plainly, God's parental training of His children is based on the foundational principles of grace that we saw in chapter 1. Our acceptance by God is always based on the righteousness of Christ. And the enabling power to grow and become more Christlike always comes to us from Christ through the Holy Spirit.

How then are you being disciplined? Is it by law, or is it by grace? Of course, God *is* disciplining by His grace, but how do you perceive it? How are you seeking to respond to His parental training? Do you accept the forgiveness of His grace, or do you labor under the burden of guilt? Are you relying on your union with Christ and the indwelling Holy Spirit for the power to respond to God's training, or is the Bible only a rule book of commands you are struggling to obey by your own willpower?

Remember, the grace that brought salvation to you is the same grace that teaches you. But you must respond on the basis of grace, not law. You must learn to depend daily on Christ for your acceptance and your power.

THINK ABOUT IT.

CHAPTER 4

THE ROLE OF
THE HOLY SPIRIT

A RE YOU READY for a couple of big words? They are *monergistic* and *synergistic*. You are probably familiar with synergistic. It describes the action of two agents working together to produce a total effect that is greater than the sum of the individual effects.

How about monergistic? What does that mean? Actually, my usually reliable Collegiate Dictionary doesn't even list the word, so I'll give you a lay person's definition. As you've probably guessed, it describes the action of a single agent working alone.

I'm not trying to play word games with you. These two words are important in understanding the role of the Holy Spirit in our spiritual growth. Monergistic describes the work the Holy Spirit does in us apart from any conscious effort on our part. Synergistic describes the work He does in us in which we participate. In monergism the Spirit works alone. In synergism He enables us to work. But whether it's the Holy Spirit working alone or enabling us to work, all spiritual growth is the result of His work. We cannot make one inch of progress apart from Him. This is the important point of this chapter.

I consider 2 Corinthians 3:18 to be one of the clearest descriptions of Christian growth we find in Scripture. The verse says, "And we all, with unveiled face, beholding the glory of the Lord, are being transformed into the same image from one degree of glory to another. For this comes from the Lord who is the Spirit" (ESV).[1]

In this passage the phrase "are being transformed into the same image from one degree of glory to another" is a description of spiritual growth. The key word is *transformed,* which in the context describes a significant and fundamental change in our inner being. This concept of growth or transformation is historically known as *sanctification.* Although I prefer the word *transformation* or the phrase *spiritual growth,* in this chapter I will bow to history and use *sanctification.*

Sanctification then is the work of the Holy Spirit in us whereby our inner being is progressively changed, freeing us more and more from sinful traits and developing within us over time the virtues of Christlike character. However, though sanctification is the work of the Holy Spirit in us, it does involve our wholehearted response in obedience and the regular use of the spiritual disciplines that are instruments of sanctification.

REGENERATION

Sanctification actually begins at the time of our conversion, when by an act called *regeneration,* or the new birth, the principle of spiritual life is planted within us. This work of regeneration is promised in such Old Testament prophecies as Jeremiah 31:33 where God says, "I will put my law in their minds and write it on their hearts." And in Ezekiel 36:26-27 He says, "I will give you a new heart and put a new spirit in you; I will remove from you your heart of stone and give you a heart of flesh. And I will put my Spirit in you and move you to follow my decrees and be careful to keep my laws."

50

In the New Testament, Paul also described regeneration in 2 Corinthians 5:17: "Therefore, if anyone is in Christ, he is a new creation; the old has gone, the new has come!" And again in Titus 3:5: "He saved us through the washing of rebirth [or regeneration, as it is translated in many versions of the Bible] and renewal by the Holy Spirit."

Notice the radical change that is described in each of these Scripture passages. God will put His law in our minds and write it on our hearts. He will give us a new disposition that, instead of being hostile to God's law, actually delights in it. The law that was merely external is now written in our hearts by the Spirit of God, so that we are moved to obedience.

The heart of stone is transformed into a heart of flesh. "Heart of stone" is a figurative expression for a hard heart, one that is insensible to the things of God and unable to receive any impressions of divine truth. The heart of flesh represents a soft and tender heart, one that is able and willing to receive and act upon the truths of God's Word.

Paul said in 2 Corinthians 5:17 that when a person is united to Christ, there is a new creation. A Christian is a radically changed person the moment he or she trusts Christ. This doesn't mean we become "saints" in practice overnight. But, it does mean a new creation—a new principle of life—has been planted within us by the Holy Spirit, and we can never be the same again.

The expression "born again" from John 3:3-8 is usually taken to mean no more than being saved from the penalty of sin. According to Jesus, it means to be born of the Spirit (John 3:6,8), that is, to be given new life. Paul said the same thing in Titus 3:5 when he spoke of renewal by the Holy Spirit. This act of regeneration or new birth by which a person enters the kingdom of God (John 3:5) is a monergistic work of the Holy Spirit. Thus it is entirely a work of grace, just as justification is.

SANCTIFICATION

Regeneration, then, is the beginning of sanctification. Sanctification is the carrying out of regeneration to its intended end. William S. Plumer, a nineteenth-century Presbyterian minister, wrote,

> Regeneration is an *act* of God's Spirit. Sanctification is a *work* of God's Spirit, consequent upon that act. . . . In regeneration we become "newborn babes;" in sanctification we attain the stature of full-grown men in Christ Jesus.[2]

The question is sometimes asked, "What is the relationship of sanctification to justification? Can a person be justified but not sanctified?" The answer is, justification and sanctification are inseparable. God never gives justification without sanctification (see 1 Corinthians 1:30 and 6:11). Both have their source in the infinite love and free grace of God. Both are accomplished by faith. In justification we rely on what Christ did *for* us on the cross. In sanctification we rely on Christ to work *in* us by His Holy Spirit. In justification, as well as regeneration, God acts alone. In sanctification He works in us but elicits our response to cooperate with Him. Quoting William Plumer again,

> Justification is an act of God complete at once and forever. Sanctification is a work of God begun in regeneration, conducted through life and completed at death. The former is equal and perfect in all; the latter is not equal in all, nor perfect in any till they lay aside the flesh. In justification God imputes [that

is, credits] to us the righteousness of Christ; in sanctification he [imparts] grace, and enables us to exercise it.[3]

Our part or our response to the Holy Spirit's work and our coopera-
tion with Him in His work is the pursuit of spiritual growth. We will
be considering our part in sanctification beginning in chapter 5. But for
now, I want to remind us that sanctification, though requiring diligent
effort on our part, is dependent upon the enabling power of the Holy
Spirit. The apostle Paul expressed this principle of dependent discipline
quite succinctly in Philippians 4:13: "I can do everything through him
who gives me strength." Paul did the work, in that case, learning to be
content. But he did it through the enabling strength of the Holy Spirit.
It is difficult to grasp this principle of synergism, of being responsible
yet dependent. But it is absolutely vital that we grasp it and live by it.

THE GOAL

The goal of sanctification is likeness to our Lord Jesus Christ. Paul
said in 2 Corinthians 3:18 that we "are being transformed into his likeness." In Romans 8:29 he said that God "predestined [all believers] to
be conformed to the likeness of his Son." Christlikeness is God's goal
for all who trust in Christ, and that should be our goal also.

Both words, *transformed* and *conformed*, have a common root, *form,*
meaning a pattern or a mold. "Being transformed" refers to the process;
conformed refers to the finished product. Jesus is our pattern or mold.
We are being transformed so that we will eventually be conformed to
the likeness of Jesus. This process is also known as spiritual formation.

Sanctification, then, is conformity to the likeness of Jesus Christ.

53

We see this same idea expressed in different wording in other New Testament Scriptures. In Ephesians 4:24, Paul said our new self is "*created to be like God* in true righteousness and holiness." The writer of Hebrews stated God disciplines us "that we may *share in his holiness*" (Hebrews 12:10), and in 1 Peter 1:16, the apostle Peter quotes an Old Testament passage where God said, "Be holy, because *I am holy*" (emphasis added in each Scripture quoted).

———

A PROCESS

We can easily see that conformity to Jesus is a lifelong process and a goal that will never be attained completely in this life. That is why Paul refers to the continual change being wrought in us with his expression in 2 Corinthians 3:18, "with ever-increasing glory," or as it is translated in the *English Standard Version,* "from one degree of glory to another." As the Spirit of God works in us, we progress from one stage of glory to the next. We are slowly but surely being changed into the likeness of Christ.

Because sanctification is a process, there will always be conflict within us between the "flesh," or the sinful nature, and the Holy Spirit. This conflict is described by Paul in Galatians 5:17: "For the sinful nature desires what is contrary to the Spirit, and the Spirit what is contrary to the sinful nature. They are in conflict with each other, so that you do not do what you want." He elaborated on this struggle in greater detail in Romans 7:14-25, where he said such things as, "I know that nothing good lives in me, that is, in my sinful nature. For I have the desire to do what is good, but I cannot carry it out" (verse 18).

I realize that not all Bible expositors regard the tension described in Romans 7:14-25 as descriptive of a normal Christian experience, let alone of someone who is vigorously pursuing holiness. Yet what honest Christian would not admit to the frequent gap between his or her spiritual desires and actual performance? Which of us would not concede that "When I want to do good, evil is right there with me" (verse 21) is a frequent lament?

The comments of John Murray are most helpful at this point. He wrote,

> The presence of sin in the believer involves conflict in his heart and life. If there is remaining, indwelling sin, there must be the conflict that Paul describes in Romans 7:14. It is futile to argue that this conflict is not normal. If there is still sin to any degree in one who is indwelt by the Holy Spirit, then there is tension, yes, contradiction, within the heart of that person. Indeed, the more sanctified the person is, the more conformed he is to the image of his Savior, the more he must recoil against every lack of conformity to the holiness of God. The deeper his apprehension of the majesty of God, the greater the intensity of his love to God, the more persistent his yearning for the attainment of the prize of the high calling of God in Christ Jesus, the more conscious will he be of the gravity of the sin which remains and the more poignant will be his detestation of it?[4]

Think of yourself walking into a room where the lighting is controlled by a dimmer switch. As you walk in, the lighting is dim and you see the furniture all in place, no newspapers lying around, and no dirty cups on the coffee table. The room looks neat and clean. But as you turn up the wattage in the lights, you begin to see dust on the furniture, smudges on the walls, chips in the paint, and threadbare spots in the carpet. The room that looked all right in the dim light suddenly appears dirty and unattractive under the full glare of the brighter light.

That is what happens in the life of a person who is growing spiritually. At first your life may appear fairly good because you've been a decent sort of person and no gross sins are visible. Then the Holy Spirit begins to "turn up the wattage" of His Word and reveal the more subtle, "refined" sins of which you were not even aware. Or perhaps you were aware of certain thoughts or actions but had not realized they were sinful.

An even better analogy might be the shining of a spotlight into the shadowy recesses of an old house. The Holy Spirit is continually shining His spotlight of conviction into the recesses of our hearts, revealing sinful attitudes and actions of which we were not aware. These newly discovered sins are usually dismaying and discomforting to us. And the more mature a person is, the more he or she is dismayed. Then as we attempt to deal with these sins, we discover that they are often stubbornly entrenched in our habits of life and are not easily dislodged. Or a sinful habit we thought had been decisively dealt with reasserts itself, and we seem powerless before its onslaught. All these experiences set up the tension within us that Paul described in the latter half of Romans 7.

Does this mean then that we are no better off than the unbeliever who struggles with some habit he or she wants to be rid of? By no means. John Murray offers helpful insight into the difference between the struggle of a believer with sin and that of an unbeliever with some undesirable habits. He wrote,

> There must be a constant and increasing appreciation
> that though sin still remains it does not have the mastery. There is a total difference between surviving sin

and reigning sin, the regenerate in conflict with sin and the unregenerate complacent to sin. It is one thing for sin to live in us: it is another for us to live in Sin.[5]

Sin is like a defeated army in a civil war that, instead of surrendering and laying down its arms, simply fades into the countryside, from which it continues to wage a guerrilla war of harassment and sabotage against the government forces. Sin as a reigning power is defeated in the life of the believer, but it will *never* surrender. It will continue to harass us and seek to sabotage our Christian lives as long as we live.

It is important for us to understand this difference between the unbeliever living complacently in sin and the believer struggling against sin. If we are going to pursue spiritual maturity, we must accept the fact that there will be continual tension within us between our desires and our performance. British theologian J. I. Packer so often says that our reach will always exceed our grasp.

THE AGENT

WE ARE NOT.

The Holy Spirit is the one responsible for this transformation. Paul said in 2 Corinthians 3:18 that we are being transformed by "the Lord, who is the Spirit." The verb *being transformed* is passive, that is, something is being done *to* us, not *by* us. This does not mean we have no responsibility in sanctification. It means that in the final analysis it is the Spirit of God who transforms us. He calls on us to cooperate synergistically and to do the part He assigns us to do, but He is the one who works deep within our character to change us. → *NOT US!*

Several passages of Scripture emphasize the fact that sanctification is primarily the work of the Holy Spirit. In 1 Thessalonians 5:23-24 Paul said, "May God himself, the God of peace, sanctify you through and through. May your whole spirit, soul and body be kept blameless at the coming of our Lord Jesus Christ. The one who calls you is faithful and he will do it." Notice that it is God Himself who will sanctify us "through and through." In other words, He will bring the process to completion.

Again Paul wrote in Philippians 1:6, "being confident of this, that he who began a good work in you will carry it on to completion until the day of Christ Jesus." Finally the writer of Hebrews prayed that God will "work in us what is pleasing to him" (Hebrews 13:21). Although these passages speak of God in a nonspecific sense, or use the pronoun *He,* we know from other Scriptures that the work of sanctification within the Trinity is primarily the work of the Holy Spirit (see 2 Thessalonians 2:13; 1 Peter 1:2). This being true, we ought to pray daily for His work of sanctification within us. One of my favorite prayers is to take the words of Hebrews 13:21 and ask that He will work in me what is pleasing to Him. (We'll look more at the place of prayer in sanctification in chapter 7.)

The Spirit of God has indeed given us certain responsibilities in the sanctifying process. In fact, the Bible is filled with exhortations, challenges, and commands to obey, as well as spiritual disciplines to be practiced. We will consider these beginning in chapter 5. However, I am now emphasizing the Spirit's work because we tend to lose sight of the fact that He is the agent of sanctification.

The way the Spirit operates in our lives to sanctify us is shrouded in mystery. Paul said He works in us "to will and to act according to his good purpose" (Philippians 2:13). But Paul never tells us just how the Holy Spirit interacts with, or works on, our human spirit. I like to know how things work, and I used to try to figure out how the Holy Spirit interacts with our spirit, but I finally realized it was a futile pursuit. On this subject the comments of John Murray are again helpful:

We do not know the mode of the Spirit's indwelling
nor the mode of his efficient working in the hearts
and minds and wills of *God's* people by which they are
progressively cleansed from the defilement of sin and
more and more transfigured after the image of Christ.[6]

We will often be conscious of the Holy Spirit's working in our lives. We will even be able to discern what He is doing to some extent, especially in those instances where He elicits a conscious response from us. But, to use the words of John Murray again, "we must not suppose that the measure of our understanding or experience is the measure of the Spirit's working."[7]

Although the Holy Spirit is the agent of sanctification and He works in us in this mysterious fashion, it is also true that He uses rational and understandable means to sanctify us. Some of these means, such as adversities and the exhortation and encouragement of others, are out-side of our control to initiate. With other means, such as the learning and application of Scripture and the frequent use of prayer, He expects us to take the initiative. We will now turn our attention to these means of growth God has given us. But as we do so, remember the "book-ends"; Christ is our righteousness, and Christ is our power.

CHAPTER 5

GROWING THROUGH THE WORD OF GOD

THE PRIMARY MEANS of growth God has given us is His Word. Peter tells us in 1 Peter 2:2 that "like newborn babies, [we should] crave pure spiritual milk, so that by it you may grow up in your salvation." Although Peter does not explicitly use a word for Scripture, five commentaries I researched all agree that "pure spiritual milk" is a metaphor for the Word of God. Just as a newborn baby is frequently hungry and cries to be fed, so we are to have a similar spiritual hunger for the Word of God that we may grow.

We saw in chapter 4 that spiritual growth is called *transformation*. Actually, the verb "transformed" is used only twice by Paul—in 2 Corinthians 3:18 and Romans 12:2. In 2 Corinthians, the emphasis is on the Spirit as the agent of transformation. In Romans 12:2, the emphasis is on the renewing of one's mind. Although the Word of God is not explicitly mentioned, it is implied as the instrument of transformation. We know the only way we can avoid conformity to the values of this world is consistent exposure to the Word of God, so that its teaching can continually influence and change our values and convictions.

So whether we think in terms of spiritual growth or spiritual transformation (two terms which actually mean the same thing), we see that the Word of God is the primary instrument that the Holy Spirit uses in our lives. This being true, it is vitally important that we have a firm conviction that the Scriptures in our Bible are indeed the very words of God to us.

THE INSPIRATION OF SCRIPTURE

The Scriptures themselves frequently assert that they are the very words of God. The purpose of this book as an introductory study to Christian growth does not allow for a detailed investigation of these claims. However, examining two key texts will help us develop the conviction that the Bible is truly God's Word to us.

The most familiar of these is 2 Timothy 3:16 which says that "all Scripture is God-breathed." Or as the ESV translates it, "all Scripture is breathed out by God." Due to the fact that the King James Version of the Bible, which was our primary English translation for 350 years, says "all Scripture is given by inspiration of God," we have come to speak of this truth as "the inspiration of Scripture." But we need to keep in mind that inspiration in that context is not the same as thinking, *Today I received inspiration from a beautiful poem.* Rather, the word refers to the fact that the Scriptures were indeed breathed out by God.

The second key text to help us is 2 Peter 1:21: "For prophecy never had its origin in the will of man, but men spoke from God as they were carried along by the Holy Spirit." We know all of Scripture was actually written by many men over a period of about 1,600 years. What Peter is telling us is that the Holy Spirit so moved upon and influenced the minds of these men as to render them the instruments of God for the infallible communication of His mind and will to us. This means that within the framework of each man's vocabulary and writing style, the Holy Spirit so guided them that they chose exactly the words and not just the thoughts that He intended them to use.

RELIABILITY AND AUTHORITY

Because the Bible is God's Word, it is both *reliable* and *authoritative*. By reliable, I mean we can trust the Bible to tell us all we need to know about God, about ourselves, and, most of all, about His plan of salvation for sinful human beings. By authoritative, I mean it expresses the will of God that we are to obey. This includes not only the moral will of God — how we should live our daily lives — but also the will of God concerning the message of salvation.

In Romans 1:5 (ESV), Paul speaks of our response to the gospel message as "the obedience of faith." Trusting in Jesus Christ as our Savior is an act of obedience to the revealed will of God just as much as loving our neighbor as ourselves.

THE INDICATIVE AND THE IMPERATIVE

Bible teachers often use two grammatical terms, *indicative* and *imperative,* and are fond of saying, "The imperative always follows the indicative." They are not referring to the structure of English grammar but to the fact that what God requires of us (the imperatives) must follow the announcement of what God has done for us through Christ Jesus (the indicatives). Obviously, in the text of Scripture, indicatives and imperatives are often intermingled. So it is *in our thinking* that the indicative must always precede the imperative. Our response to God's imperatives must always be built upon and grow out of what God has first done for us through Christ. Remember the "bookends" illustration in chapter 1. We cannot successfully put the books of God's imperatives on the shelves of our lives without first putting the bookends of His indicatives in place.

DON'T VIEW IT THIS WAY!

I learned this the hard way. When I first began to grow as a Christian, I viewed the Bible as God's rule book to guide my conduct. The indicative—the message of the gospel—was in my mind applicable only to unbelievers. I assumed as a believer I didn't need the gospel anymore except to use it as a tool for evangelism.

But I found that I do need the gospel every day, even as one who has been a Christian for more than fifty years. One mark of a growing Christian is the increasing awareness of one's sinfulness—not of the "big" sins, such as murder and sexual immorality, but of the "refined" sins of pride, a critical spirit, jealousy, resentment, selfishness, impatience, and an unforgiving spirit. All the imperatives in the world will not help me deal with those sins if I don't embrace the indicatives of the gospel: Christ is my righteousness and hence the basis of my acceptance by the Father, and Christ is the source of the power I need for dealing with those sins.

So when I say the Word of God is the primary means of growth God has given us, I am not thinking only of His moral commands intended to direct our everyday lives. We need to grow as much in our understanding of the gospel as we do in understanding the moral will of God. We'll explore this topic more in chapter 9, but I wanted to introduce it here because I want us to grasp the truth that the gospel is as important to our spiritual growth as are the moral commands of Scripture.

THE INTAKE AND INFLUENCE OF SCRIPTURE

If the Scriptures are the primary instrument of growth in our lives, how do we interact with them in such a way that they will be used by the Holy Spirit to help us grow? There are four ways we can bring ourselves under the life-changing influence of the Word of God.

The most common way is through the *teaching of others*. For most of us, that will be through the sermons of our pastors and perhaps the teaching we hear in a Sunday school class. In our day of mass communication, it may also include the tapes of messages from other speakers or radio and television teachers. The teaching of others also includes the reading of Christian books.

There are many examples of teachers in the Bible. Moses was not only the leader of the Israelites, he was also their teacher. Almost the entire book of Deuteronomy is an example of his teaching. The prophet Samuel was a teacher (see 1 Samuel 12:23). The writer of Ecclesiastes called himself "the Teacher" (Ecclesiastes 12:9-10). Paul, who was himself a teacher, wrote to Titus to "teach what is in accord with sound doctrine" (Titus 2:1). And, of course, Jesus was the Master Teacher.

As we submit our minds to the teaching of others, we want to determine as best we can that these teachers are qualified to teach, that they have been called and gifted by God and are intellectually and spiritually qualified. Another criteria we should establish before submitting our minds to someone else's teaching is this: Do they teach the Bible? This is especially needful in the area of choosing books to read. Many Christian books today are not grounded solidly in the Bible but instead represent only the thinking of the author.

Therefore, whether we are listening or reading, we should follow the example of the Berean believers who "received [Paul's] message with great eagerness and examined the Scriptures every day to see if what Paul said was true" (Acts 17:11). They were open to Paul's teaching, but they were not gullible. A radio preacher with a silver tongue or a writer with a skillful pen can be quite persuasive. But that does not necessarily mean they are teaching the truths of the Bible. What we hear and what we read must be tested against Scripture. If you do not have the ability to do this yourself, it would be good to check out your favorite radio preacher or the latest book you are reading with your pastor or another Christian who has the necessary maturity and knowledge to guide you.

The second most common way of bringing our minds under the influence of Scripture is through a *consistent Bible reading program.* Reading the Bible for yourself brings you into direct contact with Scripture. While you may not get the insights into a passage which a gifted Bible teacher can give you, your own reading gives the Holy Spirit an opportunity to impress upon your mind truths from Scripture that are particularly applicable to you at a certain time. In addition, through a regular Bible reading program, you can cover the entire Bible in a year or two and thus familiarize yourself with the whole scope of Scripture.

The purpose of our reading, of course, is to apply the Scriptures to our daily lives, not to cover so many chapters a day. Consider these instructions given by Moses for the future kings of Israel:

> When he takes the throne of his kingdom, he is to write for himself on a scroll a copy of this law . . . It is to be with him, and he is to read it all the days of his life so that he may learn to revere the LORD his God and follow carefully all the words of this law and these decrees. (Deuteronomy 17:18-19)

66

This is what we need to do. Not the writing out, of course, but the consistent reading with the intent to apply what we have read.

The third way of bringing our minds under the influence of Scripture is *Bible study*. The difference between reading and studying the Bible is a matter of intensity and depth. In reading, we gain a breadth in our knowledge of Scripture; whereas in study, we gain depth. In reading, we usually cover one to four chapters a day. In study, we will probably spend a week digging into one chapter or even a small portion. In study, we analyze the text, ask questions, compare it with other Scriptures, determine the meaning of key words, and summarize in some way our conclusions.

My own experience has shown me that Bible study is best done in small groups where each member prepares his or her study ahead of time. In that way you can profit from each other as each of you share what you have learned in your private study. A word of caution is needed at this point. All Bible study groups are not the same. They vary from ones led by people who are really teachers and do most of the talking to studies where people merely share their subjective impressions of "what the passage says to me" without having actually grappled with what the Scripture writer was saying. Look for a study where everyone does his or her homework and where the group members truly learn from each other.

A fourth means of bringing our minds under the influence of the Bible is through *Scripture memorization*. Without doubt, the classic text for Scripture memorization is Psalm 119:11: "I have hidden your word in my heart that I might not sin against you." The word "hidden" is translated as "stored up" in the ESV. This captures the meaning of the word. When I think of Psalm 119:11 now, I think of all the preparations people made in anticipation of "Y2K" as 1999 rolled into the year 2000. This, of course, turned out to be a nonevent. But beforehand, people all over the country were storing up food, water, fuel, and other necessities. They were storing them up against a time of expected future need.

This is what we do when we memorize Scripture. We store it up in our minds so it is available when we need it. It may be a promise from God, such as "Never will I leave you; never will I forsake you" (Hebrews 13:5) or a word of wisdom, such as "Do not boast about tomorrow, for you do not know what a day may bring forth" (Proverbs 27:1). Oftentimes, it will be a moral instruction, such as "Do not let any unwholesome talk come out of your mouths, but only what is helpful for building others up" (Ephesians 4:29).

When we memorize Scripture, we follow the example of Jesus. It is obvious from reading the account of Jesus' temptation by the Devil that He had memorized Scripture since He answered each of Satan's temptations by quoting a text from the book of Deuteronomy (see Matthew 4:4-10). This was not an isolated incident. As you read through the four gospels, you will note how frequently Jesus quoted Scripture. If the Son of God, in His humanity, needed Scripture stored up in His mind, how much do we?[1]

―――

KEEP YOUR EYE ON THE GOAL

I suspect by now you may be getting a bit intimidated by all I've suggested that you do to bring your mind under the influence of God's Word—particularly the idea of reading through the entire Bible, of getting involved in a Bible study that requires preparation, and then taking time to memorize key Scripture passages. It can all sound overwhelming. You may think, *I get tired just reading this chapter* and *Where does he think I'm going to get the time to do all of this?*

I understand your reaction. In this age of busyness, all of us face the pressure of more to do than we have time to do it. So we have to set some priorities. We have to determine what is most important in our lives. We have to ask ourselves, "Do I really want to grow spiritually?" If you have read this far, then I think you do want to grow. You may just feel overwhelmed at this time.

What you need to do is to get your goal clearly in mind and keep focused on that. Remember, no one has ever excelled in any professional, athletic, or musical skill without paying the price of discipline. The city where we live has in the past been the training site for a number of world-class figure skaters. I was amazed when I learned how many hours a day they spend in training. How can they keep motivated? The answer is clear. They have their eyes on the gold! They are willing to pay the price because they keep focused on the prize, although it is obvious that not many of them will ever win a medal.

Paul used the analogy of the competitive races of his day to challenge the Corinthians to pay the price of growth. This is how he put it:

> Do you not know that in a race all the runners run, but only one gets the prize? Run in such a way as to get the prize. Everyone who competes in the games goes into strict training. They do it to get a crown that will not last; but we do it to get a crown that will last forever. Therefore I do not run like a man running aimlessly; I do not fight like a man beating the air. (1 Corinthians 9:24-26)

In our case, we have an advantage over those Grecian runners. In a given race, only one received the prize, and then it was only a wreath

69

that would soon fade. But we are not in competition with anyone. We can all get the prize, and it will last forever.

What is your spiritual goal? Do you really want to get the prize? Do you want to grow to be the man or woman God wants you to be? I'm not asking do you want to be successful in a career but whether you want to be the person God wants you to be. My mother died when I was fourteen years old. She was only forty-one and had never traveled more than 200 miles from her birthplace. But while she lived, she kept her eye on the goal and she received the prize. One of her two sons became a fruitful pastor and the other one is writing this book.

By contrast, I once read of a successful businessman who was well-respected in his community and his church who, on the occasion of his seventieth birthday, wrote these words:

"My life is almost over. And despite a few cherished moments, it seems as if when I was twenty-five years old, I went to the corner store for a loaf of bread. And when I returned home, I was seventy years old."

I don't know if this man was actually a believer or merely a church member. But if he was a true Christian, his sad reflection on his life doesn't show any evidence of a desire to grow. Instead, he could only sum up his life as a trip to the corner store for a loaf of bread.

How about you? Do you want to pay the price of the spiritual disciplines you need to practice in order to grow? Or will you be content to sort of muddle through your Christian life and, at the end, have to sum it all up as no more meaningful than a trip to the corner store for a loaf of bread?

The choice is yours. What will it be?

THINK ABOUT IT.

CHAPTER 6

THE KEY TO TRANSFORMATION

I F WE ARE going to grow into Christlikeness through exposure to God's Word, one of the things we must do is to develop Bible-based convictions. A conviction is a determinative belief: something you believe so strongly that it affects the way you live. Someone has observed: A belief is what you hold, but a conviction is what holds you. You may live contrary to what you believe, but you cannot live contrary to your convictions. (This doesn't mean you never *act* contrary to your convictions, but that you do not consistently violate them.) So we are talking about the development of convictions, not mere beliefs. Convictions, of course, can be good or bad, so we want to make sure our convictions are Bible-based—that they are derived from our personal interaction with the Scriptures. How then do we develop Bible-based convictions? Let's look again at Romans 12:2.

THE INFLUENCE CONTINUUM

Do not conform any longer to the pattern of this
world, but be transformed by the renewing of your

mind. Then you will be able to test and approve what
God's will is — his good, pleasing and perfect will.
(Romans 12:2)

As we look at this Scripture, one of the first things we see is that
Paul established a contrast between conforming (or being conformed)
to the pattern of this world and being transformed by the renewal of
one's mind. He assumes there are only two alternatives: Our convictions and values will come from society around us (the world), or they
will come as our minds are renewed by the Word of God. There is no
third option.

The writer of Psalm 1 stated this truth in a similar fashion. He said,

Blessed is the man
　　who does not walk in the counsel of the wicked
or stand in the way of sinners
　　or sit in the seat of mockers.
But his delight is in the law of the LORD,
　　and on his law he meditates day and night.
He is like a tree planted by streams of water,
　　which yields its fruit in season
and whose leaf does not wither.
　　Whatever he does prospers. (Psalm 1:1-3)

The psalmist envisions two alternatives or two groups of people.
Those described in verse 1 (by way of the negative expression *does not*)
are being drawn more and more under the controlling influence of
wicked people until at last they themselves begin to influence others.
To "sit in the seat of mockers" probably refers to a position of influence and authority similar to that exercised by the teachers of the law

72

[handwritten: Second kind of people]

[handwritten: → Which one do I want to be? ← (1st group or second group)]

who "sit in Moses' seat" (Matthew 23:2). So these people are not only captive to sin themselves but influence others to sin.

The second group of people are those who delight in the law of God and meditate on it or think about it continually. Again note the psalmist presents a contrast between two diametrically opposing influences: the pervasive influence of sinful society or the life-changing influence of the law of God. There is no neutral sphere of influence. We are being influenced by the forces of sinful society, or we are being influenced by the Word of God. *[handwritten: Either HOT or COLD.]* *[handwritten: ← which one am I being influenced by?]*

The truth is, of course, that we believers are probably being influenced by both society and the Word of God. We can think of these two opposing influences as representing the two extreme ends of a continuum, as shown in the following illustration:

SINFUL SOCIETY ←——————————————→ WORD OF GOD

All of us who are believers are somewhere on that continuum, partially influenced by sinful society and partially influenced by the Word of God. The more we are influenced by society, the more we move toward the left end of the continuum. The more we are influenced by the Word of God, the more we move to the right. What determines whether we are moving to the left or to the right? The psalmist gives us the answer: our attitude toward the Word of God and the time we spend thinking about it. *Nothing else will determine where you are on that continuum.* ←

[handwritten: right = delight]

The person who is living toward the right end of the continuum is described, first of all, as one who delights in the law of God. Like the apostle Paul, this person has determined that God's law is "holy, righteous and good" (Romans 7:12). He or she sees God's law is not oner- *[handwritten: ← what?]* ous or burdensome but is given to help us please God and live lives

[handwritten: ↓ meaning of onerous]

73

that are productive and satisfying (see Psalm 1:3). One who delights in the law of God sees the Bible not just as a book of rules that are difficult to live by but as the Word of his or her heavenly Father who is the God of all grace and deals with him or her in grace.

As believers, we should be doing this. The person living toward the right end of the continuum also meditates on God's law day and night. As used in Scripture, the word *meditate* means to think about a truth with a view to its meaning and application to one's life. As God told Joshua, "Meditate on [the Book of the Law] day and night, so that you may be careful to do everything written in it" (Joshua 1:8). It is the application, or the "doing," that should be the goal of meditation. Included in this concept of meditation is reflection on one's own life to determine what conformity, or lack of it, there is between the scriptural truth and one's character or conduct. As the psalmist said, *Conforming either to the world or more like Jesus. Which one are you?*

> I have considered my ways
> and have turned my steps to your statutes.
> (Psalm 119:59)

He not only thought about Scripture. He also thought about his life and the extent to which it conformed to Scripture.

"Day and night" is an expression for *continually.* If we want to live toward the right end of the continuum of influence, our minds *deep* must be steeped in the Scriptures. We must constantly turn our minds to the Word of God, pondering the meaning and application of its truths to our lives. The idea of continual meditation may seem unrealistic and unattainable in our busy age when our minds need to be occupied with the various responsibilities we all have. "How can I meditate on Scripture," you may ask, "when I have to think about my work all day long?"

74

We should not think of the concept of "continually" as meaning every moment. Rather we should think in terms of consistently and habitually. What does your mind turn to when it is free to turn to *Ask yourself* anything? Do you begin to meditate on Scripture? I often ask people this question: "When you can think about anything you want to think about, what do you think about?" Do you think about your problems, or do you engage in mental arguing with someone else, or perhaps even allow your mind to drift into the wasteland of impure thoughts? Thinking is our most constant activity. Our thoughts are our constant occupation. We are never without them. But we can choose the direction and content of those thoughts.

Meditation on Scripture is a *discipline*. We must commit ourselves to be proactive. We must memorize key passages (or carry them on cards) so that we can think about them. We must be alert for those times during the day when we can turn our minds to the Word of God, and then we must *do* it. Even the practice of daily Bible reading *shoot!* is insufficient if we go the rest of the day without meditating on some truths of Scripture. We must choose to meditate instead of thinking about other things or listening to the radio or watching television. We simply have to decide which end of the influence continuum we want to live on and take steps accordingly. *either God or Society.*

One thing we can be sure of: If we do not *actively* seek to come under the influence of God's Word, we *will* come under the influence of sinful society around us. The impact of our culture with its heavy emphasis on materialism, living for one's self, and instant gratification is simply too strong and pervasive for us to not be influenced by it. Once again, there is no such thing as a neutral stance on the continuum of influence. We are being drawn more and more under the transforming influence of Scripture, or we are being progressively drawn into the web of an ungodly society around us.

Which one is it for you?

75

BE TRANSFORMED

The next thought we see in Romans 12:2 is that we are to be *transformed* by the renewing of our minds. We have already looked briefly at the word *transformed* in chapter 4. Transformation is much more than merely a change of outward conduct. It is a renovation of our inner being—our true self. It means our motives as well as our motivations are being changed so that we *want* to change our outward conduct.

We also saw that the verb *being transformed* in 2 Corinthians 3:18 is passive, indicating something done to us in that instance by the Holy Spirit. We noted the Holy Spirit is the transforming or sanctifying agent. We do not transform ourselves, although we do have a part to play in the process.

The verb *be transformed* in Romans 12:2 is also in the passive voice. Yet it is also an imperative—a command or, in this case, an exhortation. The use of the imperative mood with a passive verb is not common in the English language. When we give a command or urge someone to do something, we usually use an active verb. The father of a Little League baseball player will call out to his son, "Tommy, hit the ball" when he wants Tommy to do something, not have something done to him.

Yet Paul exhorts us to *be transformed*. He does not urge us to do something but to have something done to us. Another illustration with Tommy, the Little Leaguer, may help us understand what Paul was saying to us. Suppose Tommy comes in from his game all grimy with sweat and dirty from sliding into second base. His mother is preparing for guests for dinner that evening. She takes one look at Tommy and says to him, "Go take a shower."

That's a command. It is an imperative, and she uses an active verb.

76

She wants Tommy to do something. But what is the end result Tommy's mother wants? She wants Tommy to be made clean, so she directs him to take a shower. She knows Tommy cannot cleanse himself. If he tried, all he would do is rearrange the dirt. So she wants Tommy to bring himself under the cleansing action of the soap and water. It is the soap and water that will wash away the sweat and the dirt, but Tommy must bring himself under their cleansing action. So his mother says to him, "Go take a shower."

Just as Tommy cannot cleanse himself, so we cannot transform ourselves. Only the Holy Spirit can do that. But just as Tommy must bring himself under the cleansing action of the soap and water, so we must bring ourselves under the transforming action of the Holy Spirit. This means, of course, that we must continually submit our minds to the Word of God, which is the chief instrument the Holy Spirit uses to transform us.

So when Paul urged us to "be transformed by the renewing of your mind," he was essentially saying, "Bring yourself under the transforming influence of the Word of God." It is by this means that we begin to develop Bible-based convictions.

Paul's exhortation to be transformed is also in the present tense. This means we are to continue to let ourselves be transformed. It is a continuous process that should be occurring every day of our lives. As we think of our minds being renewed, we need to realize it is more than just our thoughts and understanding that need to be changed. We must also be changed in our affections and wills. But it all begins with our understanding the truth.

Therefore, we need to strive to understand it as best as we possibly can. We need to approach the Bible each day with a spirit of deep humility, recognizing that our understanding of spiritual truth is at best incomplete and to some extent inaccurate. No Christian or body of Christians has a corner on all of truth. At one time Jesus said, "I praise you, Father, Lord of heaven and earth, because you have hidden these things from the wise and learned, and revealed them to little children. Yes, Father, for this was your good pleasure" (Luke 10:21).

We need to approach the Scriptures each day as little children, asking the Holy Spirit to teach us. Regardless of how much we already know and understand, there is still an infinite storehouse of understanding of the mind of God waiting for us in Scripture. My own experience, based on fifty years of studying the Bible, is that the more I learn and understand of Scripture, the more I see how little I do understand of all God has revealed to us in His Word. So pray as the psalmist did that God will open your eyes to see wonderful things in His law and that He will give you understanding so as to keep His law (see Psalm 119:18,34). Ask the Holy Spirit to make you aware of areas of your life where you are not fully obedient to His revealed will. This is where application begins.

════

APPLY TO YOUR LIFE

Bringing ourselves under the transforming influence of the Word of God, however, means much more than just acquiring knowledge about the contents of Scripture. In fact, the mere acquisition of Bible facts or doctrinal truth without application to one's life can lead to spiritual pride. As Paul said, "Knowledge puffs up, but love builds up" (1 Corinthians 8:1). By contrast Paul also spoke of "the knowledge of the truth that leads to godliness" (Titus 1:1).

What is the difference between these two concepts of Bible knowledge? In the first instance the Corinthians were using their knowledge in a selfish and prideful way. They were "looking down their noses" at people with different convictions from theirs. On the other hand, the knowledge that leads to godliness is knowledge of the Scriptures that is being applied to one's life and results in godly behavior. ←—

One of the banes of present-day Christianity is the way we sit every week under the teaching of God's Word, or even have private devotions and perhaps participate in a Bible study group, without a serious intent to obey the truth we learn. The indictment of the Jewish people God made to Ezekiel could well be said of us today:

> My people come to you, as they usually do, and sit
> before you to listen to your words, but they do not
> put them into practice. . . . Indeed, to them you are
> nothing more than one who sings love songs with a
> beautiful voice and plays an instrument well, for they
> hear your words but do not put them into practice.
> (Ezekiel 33:31-32)

Our tendency seems to be to equate knowledge of the truth, and even agreement with it, with obedience to it. James said when we do this we deceive ourselves (see James 1:22). This is especially true when we focus on the more scandalous sins "out there" in society to the neglect of the more "refined" sins we commit.

We cannot develop Bible-based convictions merely by storing up ←— Bible knowledge in our heads. We do not even develop them by personal Bible study and Scripture memorization, though those practices certainly help us get started. As we begin to meditate on Scripture consistently, we come closer. But convictions are really developed when we begin to apply the teachings of Scripture to real-life situations.

All of life should be a theater in which we learn to apply the Word of God. Almost every event, every activity, every circumstance may be or

1. Memorize verse

2. Review, meditate, prayer, constantly asking God for application.

should be an occasion of applying a scriptural principle or even a specific verse to the situation. For starters, we can learn that we are to "always [give] thanks to God the Father for everything, in the name of our Lord Jesus Christ" (Ephesians 5:20). This is not just a nice idea; it is a spiritual imperative. Elsewhere Paul tells us that God "himself gives all men life and breath and everything else" (Acts 17:25). The scriptural principle is, God gives us everything so we should thank Him for everything.

How do we learn to apply this principle to our everyday lives? We can begin by memorizing Acts 17:25 and Ephesians 5:20. We should then for a period of time review those Scriptures daily, meditating on them, praying over them, and asking God to help us apply them to our daily lives. Begin to look for occasions throughout your day to thank God for what He has provided. As you put your socks on in the morning, thank Him that you have socks to put on. (I know that last statement may sound a bit extreme, but if you practiced it for a while, it would help you begin to learn to be continuously thankful throughout the day.) As you thank God for your food at mealtime, thank Him that He provided you or your spouse or your parents a job so the food could be bought at the local supermarket. You can even thank Him we are not living in a famine, as are other parts of the world, so there is food in the supermarket to buy.

If you are a college student, thank God as you walk to class that He has provided funds from whatever source (parents, scholarships, student loans) to enable you to be in school. You can begin to get the idea. If you do this, you will learn to see God's hand in all of life.

What about your driving? Some years ago a friend of mine began to grow spiritually. One day he read 1 John 2:6, "Whoever claims to live in him must walk as Jesus did." Since he was a "heavy-footed driver," he adapted the verse to "Whoever claims to live in him must *drive* as Jesus would." He wrote that out on a card and taped it to his

Shows how much we need God and need to know Him.

dashboard and began to apply it to his driving. Does this sound trivial? It wasn't for him. He began to apply Scripture to all of life. Today his ministry of teaching people how to apply Scripture in interpersonal relationships is literally influencing believers around the world.

Again, there is hardly a circumstance, event, or activity in all of ← your life that is not an opportunity to apply a specific verse of Scripture or at least a principle from Scripture to the situation. Even when a set of circumstances goes against our desires or frustrates our plans, we can learn to "give thanks in all circumstances" (1 Thessalonians 5:18) because "we know that in all things [that is, all circumstances] God works for [our] good" (Romans 8:28).

Hopefully, by now you get the picture. Your work, your studies, your recreation, your shopping, your driving, your interaction with other people during the day—all provide occasions for applying the Bible to your life. I cannot think of a single area or occasion of life that is not subject to the application of Scripture. If not a specific verse or verses, then a scriptural principle will apply.

Furthermore, God will in His own way bring you into circumstances where you can learn to apply His Word. For example, Paul instructs us to "bear with each other" (Colossians 3:13; see also Ephesians 4:2). To "bear with" another person means to be patient with or even overlook the unintentional faults and failures of others. Has God put you in a situation where you have frequently to interact with another person who is always late? Our Western way is to exhort that person to be on time. God's way may be for you to learn to bear with that person's fault. In fact, it is safe to say God will not want you to try to "help" that person to be on time until you have learned to be patient. God may want to change you before He changes the other person.

Most of us have had "labs" either in high school or college where we were supposed to learn to apply the theories we were learning in the classroom. The circumstances of life are our "spiritual labs" where we learn to apply what we are being taught in the "classroom" of the Bible. It is impossible, for example, for us to learn forbearance without being put in a situation where we have to bear with another's fault or failure. We can read about forbearance in the Bible. We can agree that it is something we should do as occasion requires. We can even memorize a verse such as Colossians 3:13 and meditate on it. But until we find ourselves in a circumstance that requires bearing with another person, we will not learn forbearance.

Remember, although the Bible may be the primary instrument of transformation, the Holy Spirit is the agent. So He is the One who arranges the circumstances of our lives to give us opportunity to apply Scripture. He is also the One who changes us more and more into the likeness of Jesus Christ. He is the Master Teacher. In fact, He is much more than a teacher. A teacher can only address our minds externally, but the Holy Spirit works "*in* [us] to will and to act according to his good purpose" (Philippians 2:13). Then our responsibility is to bring ourselves under His instrument—the Bible—so that He can do His work of transforming us and seek to apply in daily life what He is teaching us in the Scripture.

CHAPTER 7

DEPENDENT DISCIPLINE

A S WE SEEK to apply the Scriptures to our daily lives, we soon learn it isn't all that easy. Sure, we can train ourselves to give thanks for the socks we are putting on and the food we are about to eat, but what about doing it from the heart? What about patience with that person who is always late? Or what about those persistent sin patterns we struggle with such as anger, anxiety, discontentment, immoral thoughts, and a sharp tongue? We soon learn we need a power outside of ourselves to deal with those areas of our lives. That power, of course, is the power of Christ applied to our lives by His Holy Spirit who dwells within us. (Remember the second "bookend" of spiritual growth?) *The POWER of Christ*

There is no doubt we are responsible to grow. All the imperatives of the New Testament assume our responsibility. At the same time, we do not have the ability to grow. We are completely dependent upon the Holy Spirit. It is our duty to grow, but only the Holy Spirit can enable us to grow. It is at this point I want to introduce one of the most important principles of spiritual growth: *dependent responsibility*.

We are both responsible to grow and dependent upon the Holy Spirit to enable us to do so. This is a difficult principle to learn. We tend to vacillate between total self-effort and passive dependence. One day we "try harder," and the next day we want to just "turn it all over to the Lord and let Him live His life through us." Both approaches are wrong. As Jesus said in John 15:5, "apart from me you can do nothing." At the same time, He doesn't do the work in our place. Rather, through His Spirit, He enables us to work (see Philippians 2:12-13).

So spiritual growth very much involves our activity. But it is an activity that must be carried out in dependence on the Holy Spirit. It is not a partnership with the Spirit in the sense that we each—the believer and the Holy Spirit—do our respective tasks. Rather, we work as He enables us to work. His work lies behind all our work and makes our work possible.

What it is not.

The Holy Spirit can and does work within us apart from any conscious response on our part. He is not dependent on us to do His work. But we are dependent on Him to do our work; we cannot do anything apart from Him. In the process of spiritual growth there are certain things only the Holy Spirit can do, and there are certain things He has given us to do. For example, only He can create in our hearts the *desire* to obey God, but He does not obey for us. We must do that, but we can do so only as He gives us the enabling power to obey.

We can't do anything by ourselves.

So we must depend on the Holy Spirit to do within us what only He can do. And we must depend on Him just as much to enable *us* to do what He has given us to do. So whether it is His work or our work, in either case, we are dependent on Him. We are not just dependent on Him; we are *desperately* dependent on Him. Because we so often equate Christlike character with ordinary morality, we fail to realize how impossible it is for us to attain *any* degree of conformity to Christ by ourselves. But if we take seriously the Christlike character traits we are to put on, such as Paul lists in Galatians 5:22-23 and Colossians 3:12-14, we see how impossible it is to grow in Christlikeness apart from the influence and power of the Spirit in our lives.

Read these!

84

WORK OR PRAY?

There are many instances in the Scriptures where the concepts of both dependence and responsibility appear in the same sentence or paragraph. For example, Psalm 127:1 says,

> Unless the LORD builds the house,
>   its builders labor in vain.
> Unless the LORD watches over the city,
>   the watchmen stand guard in vain.

The psalmist sees God so intimately involved in the building and watching that he says, "Unless the Lord *builds* the house, . . . unless the Lord *watches* over the city." He does not say, "Unless the Lord *helps* the builders and the watchmen," but unless the Lord builds and watches.

Yet it is just as obvious the psalmist envisions the builders laboring to build the house and the watchmen standing guard over the city. The builders cannot put away their tools and go fishing and expect God to build the house. Neither can the watchmen retire to their beds and expect God to watch over the city. The builders must work, and the watchmen must stand guard, but they all must carry out their responsibilities in such total dependence on God that the psalmist speaks of *His* building and *His* watching.

Consider the testimony of Paul in Philippians 4:11-13:

> I am not saying this because I am in need, for I have
> learned to be content whatever the circumstances. I
> know what it is to be in need, and I know what it is to
> have plenty. I have learned the secret of being content

in any and every situation, whether well fed or hungry, whether living in plenty or in want. I can do everything through him who gives me strength. 4:13

relying on Christ. in being content

Paul said he had learned to be content. He recognized it was his responsibility to be content, and he needed to grow in that area of life. He didn't just turn it all over to the Lord and trust Him to do the work of being content. He worked at it. But he knew he could be content only through the Lord, who gave him strength. Paul also realized this strength from the Lord did not come to him as a "package sent from heaven," as if Christ's strength were a commodity to be received. Rather, he knew it came through his union with Christ, which Jesus referred to in His vine and branches metaphor in John 15:4-5. Because he was in union with Christ, he was able by faith to rely upon Christ working in him through His Spirit.

═══

THE DISCIPLINE OF PRAYER

How then can we grow in a conscious sense of dependence on Christ? Through the discipline of prayer. Prayer is the tangible expression of our dependence. We may assent to the fact that we are dependent on Christ, but if our prayer life is meager or perfunctory, we thereby deny it. We are in effect saying we can handle most of our spiritual life with our own self-discipline and our perceived innate goodness. Or perhaps we are saying we are not even committed to the pursuit of spiritual growth.

The writer of Psalm 119 teaches us about the discipline of prayer. We usually think of this psalm as the psalm of the Word of God, since God's Word is mentioned by various names in all but four of its 176 verses. But it is more accurately an expression of the psalmist's ardent desire for and commitment to obeying God. Twenty-two times the psalmist prays to God for help in obeying His law. Verses 33-37 are a good example:

> Teach me, O LORD, to follow your decrees;
>> then I will keep them to the end.
> Give me understanding, and I will keep your law
>> and obey it with all my heart.
> Direct me in the path of your commands,
>> for there I find delight.
> Turn my heart toward your statutes
>> and not toward selfish gain.
> Turn my eyes away from worthless things;
>> preserve my life according to your word.

The psalmist wants God to teach him, to give him understanding, and to direct him in the paths of God's commands. He also wants God to work directly in his heart, turning his heart toward His statutes and his eyes away from worthless things. Though he was ardent in his desire to obey, he recognized his dependence on God for doing it.

———

THE EXAMPLE OF NEHEMIAH

Our prayers of dependence should be of two types: planned periods of prayer and unplanned, spontaneous prayer. We see both of these beautifully illustrated for us in the life of Nehemiah and recorded for us in chapters 1 and 2 of that book. Nehemiah was one of the Jews in exile and was cupbearer to the Persian king Artaxerxes. The book begins with Nehemiah learning of the sad state of affairs of the Jews back in Judah and the fact that the wall of Jerusalem was broken down and its gates burned with fire. Upon hearing this, Nehemiah sat down and wept. Then he fasted and prayed for a period of several months (see Nehemiah 1).

The Scripture account doesn't indicate this, but we can assume Nehemiah set aside a certain time or times of the day during which he earnestly besought God for the welfare of Jerusalem. After all, he was the king's cupbearer and, as such, would have had official duties to perform. So most likely he would have had to schedule his times of prayer around his daily duties, just as we have to do. Since he prayed over a period of several months, we can describe this part of Nehemiah's prayer life as *planned, protracted, persevering* prayer. It was planned because it was made a part of his daily schedule, protracted because it extended over a period of several months, and persevering because he continued to pray until God answered.

One day, after several months of praying, when Nehemiah brought the king's wine to him, the king noticed that Nehemiah's face was sad. Up to this time Nehemiah had concealed his sadness of heart for his countrymen and the condition of their beloved city, Jerusalem. But now the king inquired about the cause of his sadness, and Nehemiah explained it to him (see Nehemiah 2:1-3).

Then King Artaxerxes said, "What is it you want?" (verse 4). The moment of crisis had arrived. Now Nehemiah must lay before the king his request to go to Jerusalem and rebuild its wall. But before he replied, Nehemiah "prayed to the God of heaven, and [he] answered the king" (verses 4-5). Obviously the king was not aware of Nehemiah's quick, silent prayer. It was probably something like, "Lord, help me to speak. Give me favor in the king's heart." Nehemiah sent up this quick, silent prayer to heaven even as he was opening his mouth to speak to the king. In contrast to his planned, protracted, persevering prayer over the previous few months, this prayer was *unplanned, short,* and *spontaneous.*

Both types of prayer were needed in Nehemiah's situation. Each gave validity to the other. Nehemiah didn't presume on God by waiting until that eventful day in the king's court to pray. He saw a need, ← and he persisted in prayer until God answered. At the same time, Nehemiah didn't plunge ahead to answer the king without first praying quickly and silently. He didn't presume because he had been praying for several months he didn't need to pray at that time. He was very conscious of his total dependence on God, so his quick, silent prayer was a reflex action rather than a planned one.

We can learn from Nehemiah's example how to pray for our spiritual growth. Like Nehemiah, we need to set aside time each day for *planned, protracted, persevering* prayer. We need to lay before the Lord any areas of persistent sin in our lives: sins such as gossip; irritability; impatience; lack of love; impure thoughts; and undisciplined, wandering eyes. These sins need to be the object of earnest prayer that God would work in us and *enable* us to deal with them. Note that I said, enable us. We are the ones who must deal with these sins, but the Holy Spirit must enable us to do it.

In Romans 8:13 the apostle Paul wrote, "But if by the Spirit you put to death the misdeeds of the body, you will live." Note again the dependent discipline. There is the discipline of putting to death the sins of the body that we will consider in detail in chapter 10, but we do this "by the Spirit." This means continual, fervent prayer for the work of the Holy Spirit to enable us to do what is our duty to do. We are not endowed with a reservoir of strength from which to draw. It is always "by the Spirit" that sinful deeds are put to death.

It is precisely because we are not endowed with a reservoir of strength that we need to pray daily for the Spirit's enabling work in us. Holiness requires continual effort on our part and continual nourishing and strengthening by the Holy Spirit. Unless you plan to pray, however, and set aside a specific *time* to do it, you will find you will not carry out your good intentions. So if you do not already have this practice, why not stop and make your plan now? I also find it helpful to write down on paper (for my eyes only) the specific sins I need help to deal with and the specific virtues of Christian character (more on this in chapter 11) in which, as far as I can tell, I most need to grow.

In addition to prayer about sins in our lives and areas of character in which we need to grow, it is also good to pray that we will be kept from temptation (see Matthew 6:13) and that we will be alert to and not be blindsided by temptation when it does come. Finally, in our planned time of prayer, it is good to pray along the lines of Hebrews 13:21, that God will work in us what is pleasing to Him, for He knows far better than we what really needs to happen in our lives at any given time.

Then like Nehemiah, we need those unplanned, short, spontaneous prayers. We need them throughout the day as we face temptations to sin and as we encounter circumstances in which we need help to display godly character. Whatever the situation, a simple, quick "Lord, help me" focuses our dependence upon God instead of our own willpower and brings the Spirit's aid to us. He does withhold His aid when we forget our need of it and do not ask Him for it. So we need those short, spontaneous prayers throughout the day, both to help us cultivate a sense of our dependence on Christ and to receive His aid that He sends through His Spirit.

THE SIN OF SELF-SUFFICIENCY

I believe one of the chief characteristics of our sinful nature, or "flesh" as it is called in most Bible translations, is an attitude of independence toward God. Even when we know and agree we are dependent on Him,

I am not exempt!

we tend out of habit to act independently. It is part of "the evil I do not want to do—this I keep on doing" (Romans 7:19) syndrome that clings so tightly to us. Undoubtedly, one of the reasons God allows us to fall before temptation so often is to teach us experientially that we really are dependent on Him to enable us to grow in holiness.

One of the best ways, apart from those painful experiences of failure, to learn dependence is to develop the discipline of prayer. This forces us in a tangible way to acknowledge our dependence on the Holy Spirit. This is true because, for whatever else we may say about prayer, it is a recognition of our own helplessness and absolute dependence on God.

It is this admission of helplessness and dependence that is so repugnant to our sinful spirit of self-sufficiency. And if we are naturally prone by temperament to be disciplined, it is even more difficult to acknowledge that we are dependent on Christ and His Spirit instead of on our self-discipline.

Remember, however, to become holy is to become like the Lord Jesus. And He Himself said, "By myself I can do nothing" (John 5:30). He was completely dependent on the Father, and He freely and willingly acknowledged it. His dependence was not reluctant; it was wholehearted—enthusiastic, even—because He knew we are created to be dependent on God. So if we want to grow into Christlikeness, we must pursue not a spirit of independence but a spirit of dependence. And one of the best means God has given us for doing this is the discipline of prayer.

Jesus, 12/15/12

I'm just so thankful to know you. Even reading this book, I see so much more sinfulness but looking back I also see your mercy + grace towards me. Thank you! Help me to be dependent on you and not self-sufficient. I want to be dependent on you. I [implore?]

CHAPTER 8

SPIRITUAL FELLOWSHIP

ONE DAY I received an urgent phone call from a Christian friend asking if we could have lunch together that day. We met together periodically over lunch or breakfast to share what God was doing in our lives, to encourage and counsel one another, and to share prayer requests. I was not discipling him, nor was he discipling me. We were both involved in ministering to others, but we needed and appreciated the mutual strengthening that comes from these times together.

That day, however, wasn't just an ordinary time together. My friend was hurting. Over lunch he poured out his heart to me concerning some difficult problems he was facing at work. I listened, offered a suggestion or two from the Scriptures as to how he should respond, and committed myself to pray for him. As I drove back to my office I did pray for him, and when I arrived home that evening I jotted down his need on my "emergency" prayer list.

His situation did not improve suddenly and dramatically, but over a period of several months God did answer our prayers. During that time I continued to encourage him, to pray for him, and to explore various alternatives with him until we saw God work.

This incident illustrates the importance and vital necessity of *spiritual fellowship*. Spiritual fellowship is not a social activity but a relationship of two or more believers who want to help each other grow in Christ. God has created us to be dependent both on Him and on one another. His judgment that "it is not good for the man to be alone" (Genesis 2:18) is a principle that speaks not only to the marriage relationship but also to the necessity of spiritual fellowship among all believers. None of us has the spiritual wherewithal to "go it alone" in our Christian lives. Spiritual fellowship is not a luxury but a necessity, vital to our spiritual growth and health. Biblical fellowship involves both a sharing together of our common life in Christ and a sharing with one another what God has given to us. One of the most important things we can share with one another is the spiritual truth that God has been teaching us, which might be of great help to fellow believers. J. I. Packer has an interesting insight about this type of fellowship:

> We should not . . . think of our fellowship with other Christians as a spiritual luxury, an optional addition to the exercises of private devotion. We should recognize rather that such fellowship is a spiritual necessity; for God has made us in such a way that our fellowship with himself is fed by our fellowship with fellow Christians, and requires to be so fed constantly for its own deepening and enrichment.[1]

Scripture contains a number of exhortations and examples on this subject. For example, Solomon says in Proverbs 27:17, "As iron sharpens iron, so one man sharpens another." It is in the exchange with each other of that which God is teaching us that our minds and hearts are whetted and stimulated. We learn from one another as together we learn from God.

Solomon, writing in Ecclesiastes, said, "Two are better than one, because they have a good return for their work: If one falls down, his friend can help him up. But pity the man who falls and has no one to help him up!" (Ecclesiastes 4:9-10).

Solomon intended more than simply a literal application of these truths to physical situations. In his rather picturesque way, he was emphasizing the importance of fellowship. Two are better than one, first, because of the synergistic effect: Two together can produce more than each of them working alone. Two Christians sharing the Word together can learn more than the two of them studying individually. They stimulate one another. Second, two people together can help each other up when they fall or even when they are in danger of falling. One of the many advantages of fellowship is the mutual admonishing or encouraging of one another in the face of a temptation or an attack of Satan.

The writer of Hebrews was rather emphatic about the importance of this aspect of fellowship. In Hebrews 3:13 he said, "Encourage one another daily, as long as it is called Today, so that none of you may be hardened by sin's deceitfulness." Then in Hebrews 10:24-25 he said, "Let us consider how we may spur one another on toward love and good deeds. Let us not give up meeting together, as some are in the habit of doing, but let us encourage one another—and all the more as you see the Day approaching." Note the emphasis on encouraging one another in the face of temptation and spurring one another on toward love and good deeds. We need to be kept from temptation and we need to be stimulated when our zeal for Christian duty is flagging.

The admonition of Hebrews 10:24-25—"Let us not give up meeting together"—is not fulfilled merely by attending church on Sunday morning, as is so often supposed. Rather, it is fulfilled only when we follow through with the instruction to encourage, spur on, or stimulate one another. This cannot be done sitting in pews, row upon row, listening to the pastor teach. It can only be done through the mutual interchange of admonishment and encouragement. This is not to diminish the importance of the teaching ministry of our pastors. The Bible makes it quite clear that their ministry holds a vital place in our lives (see, for example, Ephesians 4:11-12; 1 Thessalonians 4:1; 1 Timothy 3:2; 1 Timothy 5:17; 2 Timothy 4:2). But we need both the public teaching of our pastors and the mutual encouragement and admonishing of one another. It is this latter that seems to be the main thrust of Hebrews 10:24-25.

Even the apostle Paul, spiritual giant that he was, recognized his need for fellowship with other believers. Writing to the church in Rome, he expressed the desire "that you and I may be mutually encouraged by each other's faith" (Romans 1:12). He wanted to strengthen the faith of the Roman Christians, but he also wanted them to strengthen his. He constantly acknowledged his need for other believers.

Historically, the church's Apostles' Creed speaks of "the communion of saints," referring no doubt to both the objective community relationship and the experiential sharing of spiritual fellowship with one another. Packer tells us, "The Puritans used to ask God for one 'bosom friend,' with whom they could share absolutely everything and maintain a full-scale prayer-partner relationship; and with that they craved, and regularly set up, group conversations about divine things."[2]

We see, then, that the Bible teaches us the importance of spiritual fellowship and that church history affirms it. But how do we go about it? How can we have the kind of spiritual fellowship the Bible talks about?

First, spiritual fellowship with one another presupposes fellowship with God. If we are not having communion with God and learning from Him, we will have nothing to share with others. In addition, if we are not learning directly from God, we will not be alert and perceptive enough to learn from others. We will be dull of hearing.

Packer says, "Fellowship with God, then, is the source from which fellowship among Christians springs; and fellowship with God is the end to which Christian fellowship is a means."[3] Fellowship with God is indeed both the foundation and the objective of our fellowship with one another.

ask about this

Second, spiritual fellowship involves mutual commitment and responsibility. We must commit ourselves to faithfulness in getting together, openness and honesty with one another, and confidentiality in what is shared. We must assume the responsibility to encourage, admonish, and pray for one another. Spiritual fellowship means that we "watch out" for one another, feeling a mutual responsibility for each other's welfare. This does not mean that we transfer the responsibility for our Christian walk to another person or that we assume his, but rather that we help each other through encouragement and accountability.

This high level of commitment is normally made with just one person or a few selected people. Such a depth of fellowship simply cannot be maintained with every Christian, nor does God intend it. Though objectively we are in fellowship with every other believer throughout the world, in our subjective personal experience such fellowship can be maintained with only a few. We must look to God to lead us to the few special people with whom we can develop such a commitment and sense of responsibility.

As we accept the fact that spiritual fellowship with one another implies a personal fellowship with God and a mutual commitment to one another, we can then look at some practical suggestions, some specific activities that will help us experience vital fellowship with one another.

SHARING BIBLICAL TRUTH

First, we must share the truth of Scripture with one another. Spiritual fellowship should always be centered around Bible teaching. The apostle John made the truth concerning Jesus Christ the basis of his call to fellowship (see 1 John 1:1-3). I have already mentioned the synergistic effect that occurs when two or more believers share together what God is teaching them.

The psalmist said to God, "With my lips I recount all the laws that come from your mouth" (Psalm 119:13). He declared to others what God was teaching him. Through this exercise, he not only edified others but also strengthened his own understanding of God's truth. There is an old adage that says, "Words disentangle themselves when passing over the lips or through the pencil tips." As we share our thoughts with others, we learn because we are forced to organize and develop our ideas.

Some Christians feel threatened by this kind of fellowship. They feel that they have nothing to share. They are terrified by the question, "What has God been teaching you recently?" A practical way to overcome this fear of sharing is to record daily the most important truth you get from your Bible reading that day. You may want to write a sentence or a paragraph, depending on the fullness of your thinking on that particular truth. Then arrange to get together weekly with an understanding Christian friend—perhaps someone who shares your fear of sharing openly—and pass on to each other what you have learned from the Scriptures that week.

Another way to begin to share with someone is to memorize Scripture together. That is, although you must work on memorizing the verses as individuals, you can get together once a week to quote your verses to each other and share what God has taught you from those verses. As you do this on a regular basis, you will experience the iron-sharpening-iron effect described in Proverbs 27:17. Whether it comes from reading, study, or memorization of the Bible, the sharing of biblical truth with one another should be done in a way that makes it relevant to your daily life. It is not enough to tell someone what fresh insight you have gained from the Scriptures. What do those insights mean to you in a practical way? How have you grown through them? How have you applied them or how do you plan to apply them? It is the *application* of Scripture, not just the academic knowledge of it, that makes it fruitful in our lives.

Those who have learned to share easily with others what they are learning from God face the danger of failing to listen to what another Christian is saying. Too often we are so eager to share what we have learned that we fail to hear what God is saying to us through another believer. In such a case, we are not really interested in fellowship but in displaying our own knowledge of Scripture. We are playing spiritual one-upmanship. For those who have this temptation, it would be well to remember the words of Jesus when He prayed, "I praise you, Father . . . because you have hidden these things from the wise and learned, and revealed them to little children" (Luke 10:21). God may very well have something to say to us through one who speaks with stammering lips and a halting tongue. ← *ask about this.*

OPENNESS WITH ONE ANOTHER

Spiritual fellowship, however, involves more than the mutual sharing of scriptural truths. It also involves the sharing of our sins, failures, and discouragements, as well as our blessings and joys. And throughout all our spiritual fellowship we need to have a view to mutual exhortation, encouragement, and prayer. James told us, "Confess your sins to each other and pray for each other so that you may be healed" (James 5:16).

This aspect of fellowship is threatening to most of us. We hesitate to expose our sins, or even our doubts and discouragements. Our problem, of course, is pride—the fear of what another person will think of us if he knows how we have sinned. We forget that "no temptation has seized [us] except what is common to man" (1 Corinthians 10:13). Very likely the friend with whom you are seeking to have fellowship is struggling with the same temptation, or at least with another one that he or she is equally embarrassed about.

We cannot encourage, motivate, or pray for one another if we do not know the struggles the other person is facing. Remember Packer's statement about the Puritans? They asked God for a friend with whom they could share absolutely everything. We need to ask God for such a close friend. And then, after we find that friend, we need to be willing to open our lives to him or her.

ACCOUNTABILITY

Spiritual fellowship involves more than openness with one another; it also calls for mutual accountability. The ideas of admonishing one another (Colossians 3:16) and submitting to one another (Ephesians 5:21) both suggest the concept of mutual accountability. Accountability is the willingness to be both checked on and challenged in agreed-on areas of one's life. For example, if you and I have committed ourselves to spiritual fellowship, we might agree to be accountable to each other in certain disciplines: regular fellowship with the Father, Bible study, Scripture memorization, and meditation. As we meet together regularly, we give account to one another regarding our progress in those areas.

Another area of accountability is the area of so-called weaknesses. These weaknesses may be due to frailties of the temperament (such as lack of discipline in time management or lack of self-control), or they may be due to "besetting sins," those temptations to which we are particularly vulnerable. If you are struggling with a temperament weakness or a particularly compelling temptation, you need to be willing to share those problems with someone you are close to in the Lord. Asking for that person's prayer support and voluntarily becoming accountable to him will provide you with great strength in overcoming that weakness or resisting that temptation.

PRAYING TOGETHER

The fourth ingredient of fellowship is praying with and for one another. The Puritans not only wanted someone with whom they could share absolutely everything, but they also wanted a person with whom they could maintain a full-scale prayer-partner relationship.

Oftentimes we have prayer needs that are not appropriate for sharing in our local congregations or campus ministry groups, or even in our small group Bible studies. But we can share these needs with our "bosom friend." No prayer request should seem so insignificant or embarrassing that we would not feel free to mention it to the friend with whom we have intimate spiritual fellowship.

I have already mentioned the twofold concept of commitment and responsibility. If I have made a mutual commitment with and assumed a spiritual responsibility for someone else, that responsibility cannot be fulfilled without the mutual dedication to prayer. God works in another person's life largely as a result of prayer. He may use my sharing from the Scriptures and my words of admonishment and encouragement, but

He does so as a result of my prayers. My own study of the Scriptures, verified by personal experience, has convinced me that prayer is the most important ministry I can have in the life of another individual. So if I truly want to have a close spiritual relationship with another believer, I must commit myself to pray for him.

═══

QUALIFICATIONS FOR FELLOWSHIP

As you become convinced of the importance and necessity of spiritual fellowship with other believers on a close personal level, you will begin to ask: "Who can I have this kind of fellowship with?" It is obvious from what we have considered about mutual commitment, openness of sharing, and willingness to give and receive both encouragement and admonishment that you are not going to enter into this kind of relationship with just anyone in the body of Christ. There are certain qualifications that both of you must meet. Here are some qualities to look for as you ask God for a bosom friend:

- A desire, backed up by action, to grow in the Lord, both in personal character and in ministry to others.
- An ability to understand and identify with your needs, frustrations, and temptations, but in an objective way. We need understanding, but not pity.
- An ability to absolutely keep confidences so that you can share your inmost heart.
- A willingness to make a commitment toward your spiritual welfare.
- A mature recognition that he or she does not have all the answers for your life; a willingness to agonize, pray, and search the Scriptures with you for those answers.

- A willingness to be honest with you, not allowing you to continue unchallenged in a wrong attitude or action.

Those who are just beginning to grow in their Christian faith should look first for this kind of fellowship from someone who can disciple them on a one-to-one basis. A peer-level fellowship can be helpful to a young Christian for encouragement and prayer, but it should be accompanied by a fellowship environment that can provide a strong commitment to growth in understanding and application to the Scriptures. Christians who are more mature in the Lord will likely find their spiritual fellowship on a peer level with others of similar spiritual maturity.

FELLOWSHIP IN SMALL GROUPS

Thus far our discussion of spiritual fellowship has focused primarily on a one-to-one relationship. This, of course, is the most basic unit of spiritual fellowship, but not the only one. Another common fellowship unit is the small group. Many small groups today are organized around Bible study. Other small groups are called "care groups," where the objective is to share needs and pray for one another. Still other groups focus on accountability, keeping each other sharp in different areas of need. Ideally, fellowship groups should seek to incorporate all of these aspects: Bible study, sharing of needs, accountability, and prayer for one another.

I have already referred to the synergistic effect of two people sharing together what they have learned from Scripture. In a small group this can be greatly multiplied as more ideas are brought to bear on a passage. This assumes, of course, that each group member is depending on the Holy Spirit to open his understanding. Certainly we are going to gain no true insights into the Scriptures apart from His ministry, regardless of how we may stimulate one another's thinking.

There is a great deal of material in print about small groups, so it is not the purpose of this book to go into detailed instruction about that subject. However, my own experience compels me to include this one word of caution: Great care should be taken to ensure that small groups do indeed accomplish the objective of spiritual fellowship, that is, of mutually enhancing our relationship with God. The dangers of spiritual pride over the knowledge we have gleaned from our Bible study and of playing one-upmanship are far greater in the small group than in a one-to-one relationship. There is also the danger of sharing strictly on an intellectual level rather than on the deeper heart level where God's Word is made applicable to our daily lives.

Spiritual fellowship becomes more and more difficult as a group becomes larger. There is obviously less intimacy and consequently less freedom to share with others what is really happening in our lives. An old Puritan adage addresses the importance of seeking to maintain fellowship with only a few in this manner: "Have communion with few, be intimate with *one*. Deal justly with all, speak evil of none."

The godly Puritans, who changed the face of English history amid unusual difficulties, realized the importance of genuine spiritual fellowship, the type mentioned by the writer of Hebrews. Most of the Puritan era was characterized by persecution of godly ministers and their ejection from their churches. They often ministered to their flocks in the woods outside the towns so as to avoid harassment from their enemies. It was vitally necessary in such difficult times for them to encourage each other and to spur each other on. Fellowship to them was no luxury; it was an urgent necessity.

We need to consider carefully, then, their advice about the *breadth* of fellowship. They realized that for fellowship to have depth in its meaning, it must be limited in its breadth: communion with a few, intimacy with one. Fellowship beyond the few tends to take on superficial characteristics, leading to little more than Christian social relationships that have erroneously become characterized as fellowship. Perhaps we need to take more literally the small number indicated by Jesus in that well-known passage, "Where two or three come together in my name, there am I with them" (Matthew 18:20). It is not, of course, that Christ is absent from us in our larger assemblies. Yet He does particularly emphasize in this statement the importance of the small fellowship group.

GOD'S DELIGHT IN FELLOWSHIP

Right at the end of the Old Testament we get a glimpse into the heart of God and His value of spiritual fellowship among believers. The setting is the nation of Israel in the process of being restored to its land by the Persian king, but falling again into a corrupt religious formality, neither worshiping nor obeying God. In fact many people of Israel were even saying that it was futile to serve God (see Malachi 3:14-15).

Yet in the midst of that spiritual declension there was a group who feared the Lord and had fellowship together: "Those who feared the LORD talked with each other, and the LORD listened and heard. A scroll of remembrance was written in his presence concerning those who feared the LORD and honored his name" (Malachi 3:16). Two things are apparent from this passage concerning fellowship: (1) The godly Jews considered fellowship important. No doubt they had learned the vital necessity of encouraging one another in those difficult days of national backsliding. (2) But just as important is the clear indication of God's delight in their fellowship. He listened in on their times of fellowship, took special note of it, and even had a "scroll of remembrance" written in His presence concerning these godly people who sought to encourage one another and build each other up in the fear of the Lord.

The infinite, eternal mind of God obviously does not need a scroll of remembrance to remind Him of the gracious acts of His people. The allusion to such a scroll is for our benefit, that we might see the importance God places on true spiritual fellowship among His people and the delight it brings to His heart.

If you and I are going to grow spiritually, we cannot play "Lone Ranger." We must incorporate spiritual fellowship into our Christian lives.

CHAPTER 9

THE INSTRUMENT
OF THE GOSPEL

A S WE CONSIDER the various means or instruments of growth the Holy Spirit uses, it may surprise you I would include the gospel. We can readily understand the use of Scripture, prayer, and the fellowship of other believers. But where does the gospel fit in? To answer that question, we need to look again at 2 Corinthians 3:18, one of the key verses on Christian growth: "And we all, with unveiled face, beholding the glory of the Lord, are being transformed into the same image from one degree of glory to another. For this comes from the Lord who is the Spirit" (ESV). In this verse Paul draws a connection between our beholding the glory of the Lord and our being transformed.

What is the glory of the Lord that Paul referred to, and how does beholding it transform us? First, the glory of the Lord denotes the presence of God and all that He is in all of His attributes—His infiniteness, eternalness, holiness, sovereignty, goodness, and so on. In other words, God is glorious in all of His being and all of His works. However, in the context of 2 Corinthians 3:18, Paul was contrasting the glory of the law given by Moses with the far-surpassing glory of the gospel (see 2 Corinthians 3:7-11). Then in 2 Corinthians 4:4, he spoke of "the gospel of the glory of Christ." This means the glory of Christ is good news, for the word gospel means good news.

This close connection between the gospel and Christ's glory leads me to believe that Paul was in this instance thinking of the glory of Christ, especially as it is revealed in the gospel. The law reveals the glory of God in His righteousness; the gospel reveals the glory of God in both His righteousness and grace. Christ's death reveals the righteousness of God in that it satisfied the justice of God, but it also reveals the grace of God in that it was the means of salvation to those who deserve only eternal wrath.

It seems that God desires to magnify His grace in a special way to us, for Paul wrote in Ephesians 2:6-7,

> And God raised us up with Christ and seated us with
> him in the heavenly realms in Christ Jesus, in order
> that in the coming ages he might show the incompa-
> rable riches of his grace, expressed in his kindness to
> us in Christ Jesus.

The key phrase is that God might show the incomparable riches of His grace. This is God's goal in salvation of fallen human beings: the exaltation of His grace shown to us in Christ.

James Fraser (1700-1769), an obscure Scottish pastor, wrote a masterful treatise on sanctification that was recognized as a classic in its day and has been reprinted. He has this to say about the glory of the gospel:

> It is the gospel that exhibits God's highest glory,
> which he chiefly designs to display before sinful men,
> even that glory of God that shineth in the face of
> Christ. It is the gospel that sets forth the glory of

Christ, and by which the Holy Spirit himself is glorified; and it is it that will be honoured with the
[accompanying] influence of the Holy Spirit.[1]

This then is the glory that has a transforming effect on us. It is the
glory of Christ revealed in the gospel, the good news that Jesus died in
our place as our representative to free us not only from the penalty of
sin but also from its dominion. A clear understanding and appropriation of the gospel, which gives freedom from sin's guilt and sin's grip,
is, in the hands of the Holy Spirit, a chief means of spiritual growth.

To the degree we feel we are on a legal or performance relationship with God, to that degree our progress is impeded. A performance
mode of thinking gives indwelling sin an advantage because nothing
cuts the nerve of the desire to grow as much as a sense of guilt. On the
contrary, nothing so motivates us to want to grow as does the understanding and application of the two truths that our sins are forgiven
and the dominion of sin is broken because of our union with Christ.

In the words of Hebrews 9:14, it is "the blood of Christ" that will
"cleanse our consciences from acts that lead to death [that is, from sinful acts], so that we may serve the living God!" We cannot serve God
or pursue spiritual growth with any vigor at all if we are dealing with a
guilty conscience. Therefore we need the gospel to remind us that our
sins are forgiven in Christ and "the blood of Jesus, his Son, purifies us
from all sin" (1 John 1:7).

Our specific responsibility in the pursuit of growth as seen in 2 Corinthians 3:18 then is to behold the glory of the Lord as it is displayed in
the gospel. The gospel is the "mirror" through which we now behold
His beauty. One day we shall see Christ, not as in a mirror, but face
to face. Then "we shall be like him, for we shall see him as he is"
(1 John 3:2). Until then we behold Him in the gospel. Therefore, we

must keep the gospel continually before us. Always keep in mind the first "bookend" of Christ's righteousness. To behold the glory of Christ in the gospel is a discipline. It is a habit we must develop by practice as we learn to bathe our minds in the gospel. None of the means of growth is more important than beholding the glory of Christ in the mirror of the gospel and experiencing the conscience cleansing effect of the blood of Christ.

WE DIED TO SIN

"But," someone may ask, "doesn't the continual emphasis on the gospel and the free pardon of our sins open the door to 'easy believism'— the idea that now that I've prayed a prayer and 'been saved' from eternal punishment, it doesn't matter how I live?" Paul anticipates such a question in Romans 6:1. In response to his statement in Romans 5:20, "But where sin increased, grace increased all the more," he himself raises the objection: "What shall we say then? Shall we go on sinning so that grace may increase?" If we are justified freely by God's grace through the work of Christ, doesn't more sin increasingly magnify God's grace?

"By no means!" responds Paul. "We died to sin; how can we live in it any longer?" (Romans 6:2). Paul's response is not an impatient "How could you think such a thing?" Rather, as he demonstrates in the following verses, such a practice cannot occur because a fundamental change has occurred in our relationship to sin. The expression Paul uses for this decisive change is, "We died to sin."

Now here is the difficult part. What does Paul mean when he says that we died to sin? It's fairly obvious he does not mean that we died to the daily committal of sin. If that were true, no honest person could claim to be justified, because we all sin daily (as we saw in chapter 2). Nor does it mean that we died in the sense of being no longer responsive to sin's temptations. If that were true, Peter's admonition to abstain from sinful desires (see 1 Peter 2:11) would be pointless. So what does Paul mean?

Conservative evangelical commentators have generally taken one of two positions in answering this question. Several have held that Paul refers exclusively to the *guilt* of sin. That is, through our union with Christ in His death, we died to sin's guilt. This view would seem to be consistent with Paul's statement in Romans 7:4 that through Christ we died to the Law—not to the law as an expression of God's moral will but to the condemnation and curse of the Law. To say we died to the guilt of sin and to the condemnation of the Law addresses the same issue.

Other commentators say that Paul means we died to the *reign* and *dominion* of sin in our lives. In other words, because sin no longer exercises absolute dominion over us, we no longer *can* (speaking of ability) continue in sin as a predominant way of life. We struggle with sin, and we do sin, but sin no longer is our master. In the opinion of these commentators, this is the only view that addresses Paul's question, "Shall we go on sinning so that grace may increase?"

I believe both views should be brought together. *The guilt of our sin in Adam resulted in our being given over to sin's dominion as a penal consequence.* When a judge sentences a person convicted of a crime to five years in prison, that sentence is the penal consequence of the crime. That is analogous to what God did to Adam and all his posterity. Part of the penal consequence of Adam's sin was to be delivered over to the dominion or bondage of sin. That is why David said, "Surely I was sinful at birth, sinful from the time my mother conceived me" (Psalm 51:5).

In the case of the prisoner who has served his five years, his penal consequences are over. The broken law no longer has a claim against him. In that sense he has ended his relationship to the law and its penal consequences. He must continue to obey the law in the future, but the particular offense that sent him to prison has been dealt with forever. To use Paul's expression, he has died to the law and its penal consequences.

How does this apply to us? Let me paraphrase from the comments of John Brown, a nineteenth-century Scottish pastor, theologian, and author of several commentaries:

> The wages of sin is death. Until the condemning sentence is executed, a person is subject to sin, both in its power to condemn and its power to deprave [or exert dominion]. But let the penal consequences be fully endured, let the law's penalty be fully paid, and the person is at once delivered from sin's condemning power and its depraving influence or dominion. It is in this way that all that are in Christ Jesus, all that have been justified by His grace, have died, not in their own persons, but in the person of their Surety. They are therefore delivered from the reign of sin — from its power to condemn, and therefore, also from its power to rule in the heart and life.[2]

COUNT YOURSELVES DEAD TO SIN

So we are free from both the guilt and the reigning power or dominion of sin in our lives. Of what use is this information to us? How can it help us when we are struggling with some persistent sin pattern and see ourselves often giving in to our sinful desires? Here is where Paul's instructions in Romans 6:11 can help us: "In the same way, count yourselves dead to sin but alive to God in Christ Jesus."

It is important we understand Paul's point because he is not telling us to *do* something but to believe something. We are to count on, or believe, that we are dead to sin. First of all, we are dead to its guilt. God no longer counts it against us. We are no longer under condemnation because of it (see Romans 4:8; 8:1).

This is not make-believe. You are indeed guilty in yourself, but God no longer regards you as guilty because the guilt of your sin has already been borne by Christ as your substitute. The sentence has been served. The penalty has been paid. To use Paul's expression, you have died to sin's guilt.

William Romaine (born 1714) was one of the leaders of the eighteenth-century revival in England, along with George Whitefield and the Wesley brothers. In his classic work on faith he wrote,

> No sin can be crucified either in heart or life, unless
> it be first pardoned in conscience, because there will
> be want of faith to receive the strength of Jesus, by
> whom alone it can be crucified. If it be not mortified
> in its guilt, it cannot be subdued in its power.[3]

What Romaine was saying is that if you do not believe you are dead to sin's guilt, you cannot trust Christ for the strength to subdue its power in your life. So the place to begin in dealing with sin in your life is to count on the fact that you died to its guilt through your union with Christ in His death. This is an important truth you need to ponder and pray over until the Holy Spirit convinces you of it in both your head and heart.

DO NOT LET SIN REIGN

We have, however, died not only to sin's guilt but also to its reigning power in our lives. Here sin is viewed as an active principle that seeks to dominate us. As an analogy to help us understand, the will to live is an active principle within us. With few exceptions, that principle always asserts itself when we are faced with a life-threatening situation. We instinctively fight to save our lives.

Now, although sin as an active principle is still with us, it can no longer reign supreme in our lives. We are united to Christ, and His Holy Spirit has come to reside in us. We have been delivered from the power of Satan and given a new heart (see Ezekiel 36:26; Acts 26:18). However, as believers we do experience the tension Paul describes in Galatians 5:17: "For the sinful nature desires what is contrary to the Spirit, and the Spirit what is contrary to the sinful nature. They are in conflict with each other, so that you do not do what you want."

George Smeaton described the tension this way:

> There [is] an internal conflict between flesh and spirit
> between an old and new nature. And the strange
> thing is, that in this conflict the power and faculties
> of the Christian seem to be occupied at one time by
> the one, and at another time by the other. The same
> intellect, will, and affections come under different
> influences, like two conflicting armies occupying the
> ground, and in turn driven from the field.[4]

Another way of describing this tension between the sinful nature and the Spirit is to liken it to a tug-of-war. With two opposing teams pulling on the rope, its direction of movement often goes back and forth until one team eventually prevails. This is the way it will be with us until the Holy Spirit finally prevails.

We must acknowledge this tension if we are to make progress in the Christian life. Indwelling sin is like a disease that we can't begin to deal with until we acknowledge its presence. But in the case of sin, we must also count on the fact that, though it still resides in us, it no longer has dominion over us. As Paul said, "For sin shall not be your master, because you are not under law, but under grace" (Romans 6:14).

Therefore, because we have the assurance that sin shall not be our master, we are not to let it reign in our mortal bodies so that we obey its evil desires (see Romans 6:12). Rather we are, by the enabling power of the Spirit, to put to death the misdeeds of the body" (Romans 8:13), and "to abstain from sinful desires, which war against our souls" (1 Peter 2:11). Indeed, we are called to an active, vigorous warfare against the principle of sin that remains in us.

====

CHRIST'S POWER, NOT OURS

However, we are not to wage this warfare in the strength of our own willpower. Instead, as we have already seen in chapter 7, we are to look to Him by faith for the enabling power to live the Christian life. We believers are spiritually united to Christ in such a way that our spiritual life and the power to live that life comes from Him. We are not completely passive, however, in this relationship. Rather we are to abide or remain in Him by faith. That is, we are to *actively* rely on Christ for the enabling power we need to wage war against the sin that remains in us, to put on the positive virtues of Christlike character (called the *fruit of the Spirit* in Galatians 5:22-23), and to serve Christ effectively in all that He calls us to do.

PROGRESSIVE SANCTIFICATION

Warring against the sin that remains in us and putting on Christlike character is usually called *sanctification*. It is helpful, however, to speak of Christian growth as *progressive sanctification*. The word *progressive* indicates growth or positive change. To return to the tug-of-war analogy, it assumes that, though the rope may move back and forth, over time it moves in the right direction until finally we win the tug of war against sin at the end of our lives.

There is no doubt that the tug-of-war rope must move in the right direction. However, we can always expect resistance. To stay with the analogy, although the Spirit who dwells within us is stronger than the sinful nature, that nature continues to "dig in its heels" every step of the way. And sometimes it will pull the rope in the wrong direction.

What is it then that will keep us going in the face of this internal conflict? The answer is: the gospel. It is the assurance in the gospel that we have indeed died to the guilt of sin—that there is no condemnation for us who are in Christ Jesus; that the Lord will never count our sins against us; and that we are truly delivered from the reigning power of sin—that will motivate us and keep us going even in the midst of the tension between the Spirit and the sinful nature.

Paul said, "For Christ's love compels us" (2 Corinthians 5:14). To be compelled is to be highly motivated. We are to be motivated by Christ's love for us. And where do we learn of His love? Where do we hear Him say, "I love you"? It is in the gospel. The gospel, received in our hearts at salvation, not only frees us from the guilt of sin but also from the reigning power of sin. And the gospel believed every day is the only enduring motivation to pursue our warfare with sin. That is why we need to always keep the gospel before us.

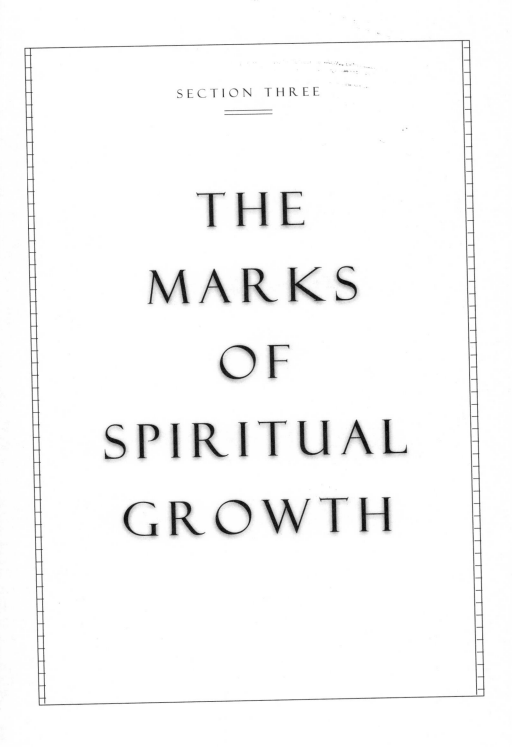

THE
MARKS
OF
SPIRITUAL
GROWTH

CHAPTER 10

THE PURSUIT
OF HOLINESS

U P TO THIS point, we have been considering the *importance* of spiritual growth and the *means* of growth. Now we want to look at some of the *marks* or characteristics of a growing Christian. There are no doubt many identifying marks, but in this book we are going to look at five that are fundamental to all the rest.

One of the first identifying marks of a growing Christian is *the pursuit of holiness*. God has called every Christian to a holy life. There are no exceptions to this call. It is not a call only to pastors, missionaries, and a few dedicated Sunday school teachers. Every Christian, whether rich or poor, learned or unlearned, influential or unknown, is called to be holy. The powerful politician and the struggling student, the wealthy professional and the shoe store clerk are all alike called to be holy.

This call to holiness is based on the fact that God Himself is holy. Peter wrote, "But just as he who called you is holy, so be holy in all you do; for it is written: 'Be holy, because I am holy'" (1 Peter 1:15-16). Because God is holy, He requires that we be holy.

What is holiness? Is it obeying a lot of rules or wearing a certain style of dress? As the above Scripture suggests, holiness is conformity to the character of God. God has called us to be like Him.

The basic meaning of holy is *separate*. When used of God, it denotes first of all that God as Creator is separate from and above all His creatures. He is the Creator; we are His creatures. Even though God created us in His image, we are still dependent upon Him, while He is totally independent and infinitely above us. The expression *transcendent majesty* best describes this aspect of God's holiness. Obviously we cannot be like God in this manner.

However, God is separate not only from His creation but especially from sin. We call this aspect of God's holiness His moral purity. God cannot have anything to do with sin. He cannot be tempted to sin, nor does He ever excuse or overlook any sin we commit, however small it may be. In fact, the Bible says that God hates sin (see Zechariah 8:17 and Hebrews 1:9). This is the sense in which we are called to be holy as He is holy.

When God calls us to be holy, He calls us to separate ourselves from sin. Paul wrote to the Corinthians to "*purify* ourselves from everything that contaminates body and spirit, perfecting holiness out of reverence for God." The writer of Hebrews exhorts us to "*throw off* everything that hinders and the sin that so easily entangles." And Peter urges us "to *abstain from* sinful desires which war against [our] souls" (2 Corinthians 7:1, Hebrews 12:1, 1 Peter 2:11, emphasis added). *Purify, throw off,* and *abstain from* are all expressions denoting what it means to separate ourselves from sin.

The apostle John wrote,

> Do not love the world or anything in the world. If
> anyone loves the world, the love of the Father is not
> in him. For everything in the world—the cravings
> of sinful man, the lust of his eyes and the boasting of

what he has and does — comes not from the Father
but from the world. (1 John 2:15-16)

Here again, we see a strong encouragement to separate ourselves
from sin, expressed by John as "Do not love the world or anything in
the world." To pursue holiness is to take aggressive action to separate
ourselves both from the sin within us: pride, selfishness, a critical
and judgmental spirit, irritability, impatience, sexual lust, and so on,
and also to take steps to separate ourselves from the ever-encroaching
temptations of society around us.

This does not mean we are to separate ourselves socially from the
world but from the sinful influences of the world. We are to be in the
world but not swayed by the world. As Paul wrote, "those who use the
things of the world, as if not engrossed in them" (1 Corinthians 7:31).

How then do we go about pursuing holiness? Actually, all I have
written up to this point is relevant. The foundation of the gospel,
the role of the Holy Spirit, the renewal of our minds by the Word of
God, the application of Scripture to everyday life, a dependent spirit
expressed through prayer, and the mutual help of fellow believers all
play a part in the pursuit of holiness.

Since the pursuit of holiness, however, involves a vigorous effort
to separate ourselves from sin within and without, there is one further
area we need to explore — the matter of our daily choices. Life is a constant series of choices from the time we arise in the morning until we
go to bed at night. Many of these choices have moral consequences. For
example, the route you choose to drive to your work each morning is
probably not morally significant, but the thoughts you choose to think
while you are driving and the way you choose to drive are moral choices.

The pursuit of holiness involves a constant series of such choices.
We choose in every situation which direction we will go, toward sin or

toward holiness. It is through these choices we develop Christlike habits of living. Habits are developed by repetition, and it is in the arena of moral choices that we develop spiritual habit patterns.

We see this development of moral habits in one direction or the other in Romans 6:19, "Just as you used to offer the parts of your body in slavery to impurity and to ever-increasing wickedness, so now offer them in slavery to righteousness leading to holiness." The believers at Rome had formerly offered the parts of their bodies to impurity and to ever-increasing wickedness. The more they sinned, the more they were inclined to sin. They were continually deepening their habit patterns of sin simply through their practice of making sinful choices. Paul urged them to make *right* choices, which would over time lead to *holy* character.

What was true of the Romans can be just as true of us today. Sin tends to cloud our reason, dull our consciences, stimulate our sinful desires, and weaken our wills. Because of this, each sin we commit reinforces the habit of sinning and makes it easier to give in to that temptation the next time we encounter it. On the other hand, making right choices tends to strengthen our resolve against sin. That's why the right choices are so important.

TRAIN YOURSELF IN THE RIGHT DIRECTION

In 1 Timothy 4:7, Paul exhorted Timothy to "train yourself to be godly." The word *train* Paul used is a word from the athletic arena, a word used to describe the training activity of young men as they prepared themselves to compete in the athletic games of that day. Just as those young men trained themselves physically in order to compete in the games, so Paul wanted Timothy, and now us, to train ourselves spiritually toward godliness. Though godliness is a broader concept than holiness (see chapter 11), holiness is a major part of it, so training ourselves to be godly certainly includes training ourselves in holiness.

The important point, however, is that we train ourselves through exercise. In fact, the *King James Version* translates this phrase as, "exercise thyself rather unto godliness." And how do we exercise ourselves in the spiritual realm? Through the choices we make.

What happens when we make wrong choices, when we choose to sin instead of obey God's Word? We train ourselves in the wrong direction. We reinforce the sinful habits we have already developed and allow them to gain greater strength in our souls.

Consider 2 Peter 2:14: "With eyes full of adultery, they never stop sinning; they seduce the unstable; they are experts in greed—an accursed brood!" This is part of the apostle Peter's description of false teachers, and in verse 14 we are right in the middle of it. The key phrase in verse 14 for our present purpose is, "they are experts in greed." The *English Standard Version* says they have "hearts trained in greed." The word *trained* is the same verb Paul used when he wrote, "train yourself to be godly." Peter said the false teachers had *trained* themselves to be greedy. They had trained themselves to the point where, in the very colorful but accurate expression of the *New International Version*, they had become "experts in greed."

These false teachers had become experts but in the wrong direction. Instead of becoming experts in generosity and self-giving sacrifice, they had become experts in greed. Instead of training themselves to be godly, they had trained themselves to be greedy. The word translated as "train" in the *New International Version* can just as accurately be translated as "discipline." So these false teachers were disciplined but in the wrong direction.

The message implied in 2 Peter 2:14 is very sobering. It is possible to discipline ourselves in the wrong direction. We usually think of disciplined people as those who "have their act together" and do the things they should do when they should be done. But the truth is, we are all disciplined to some degree. The question is, *In which direction are we disciplined?* Every day in some areas of life, we are disciplining ourselves in one direction or the other by the choices we make.

THE DISCIPLINE OF MORTIFICATION

Making the right choices to obey God rather than the desires of our sinful natures necessarily involves the discipline of mortification. Mortification is an archaic word we don't use much anymore, but it's one we need to resurrect. To mortify means to deny our sinful desires or, in the words of our modern Bible translations, "to put to death" those sinful desires.

The apostle Paul said in Romans 8:13: "For if you live according to the sinful nature, you will die; but if by the Spirit you put to death [mortify] the misdeeds of the body, you will live." The misdeeds of the body are the sinful actions we commit in thought, word, or deed. Paul was more explicit about these misdeeds in Colossians 3:5: "Put to death, therefore, whatever belongs to your earthly nature: sexual immorality, impurity, lust, evil desires and greed, which is idolatry." This list of sinful deeds is not meant to be complete but is only typical of the expressions of sin Paul had in mind when he said to put them to death. If we are going to pursue holiness—that is, take steps to separate ourselves from sin—we must mortify our sinful desires.

HOW TO PUT SIN TO DEATH

How then do we mortify or put to death the misdeeds—the sinful expressions—of the body? First of all, Paul did not say to mortify indwelling sin, but rather *sins,* which are the various expressions of indwelling sin. We cannot eliminate indwelling sin in this life. It will be with us until the day we die. Rather, we are to mortify specific sin patterns, which are the expressions of indwelling sin.

To mortify a sin means to *subdue* it, to *deprive it of its power,* to break the habit pattern we have developed of continually giving in to the temptation to that particular sin. The *goal* of mortification is *to weaken the habits of sin* so that we make the right choices.

First then, mortification involves dealing with all known sin in one's life. Without a purpose to obey all of God's Word, isolated attempts to mortify a particular sin are of no avail. An attitude of *universal* obedience in every area of life is essential. As Paul wrote to the Corinthians, "Let us purify ourselves from *everything* that contaminates body and spirit" (2 Corinthians 7:1, emphasis added). We cannot, for example, mortify impure hearts if we are unwilling to also put to death resentment. We cannot mortify a fiery temper if we are not also seeking to put to death the pride that so often underlies it. Hating one particular sin is not enough. We must hate all sin for what it really is: an expression of rebellion against God.

Second, not only must there be a universal fight against sin; there must also be a constant fight against it. We must put sin to death continually, every day, as the flesh seeks to assert itself in various ways in our lives. No believer, regardless of how spiritually mature he or she may be, ever gets beyond the need to mortify the sinful deeds of the body. We must make it our business, as long as we live, to mortify the sin that so easily entangles us.

Third, to mortify sin we must focus on its true nature. So often we are troubled with a persistent sin only because it disturbs our peace and makes us feel guilty. We need to focus on it as an act of rebellion against God. Our rebellion is of course against the sovereign authority of God. But it is also rebellion against our heavenly Father who loved us and sent His Son to die for us. God our Father is grieved by our sins. Genesis tells us that when "The LORD saw how great man's wickedness on earth had become. . . . The LORD was grieved that he had made man on the earth, and his heart was filled with pain" (Genesis 6:5-6). Your sin and my sin are not only acts of rebellion; they are acts that grieve God. And yet, He sent His Son to die for those very sins that fill His heart with pain.

MORTIFY YOUR SINFUL DESIRES

We must also realize that in putting sin to death we are saying no to our own desires. Sin most often appeals to us through our desires or what the older writers called our affections. Not all desires, of course, are sinful. We can desire to know God, to obey Him, and to serve Him. There are many good, positive desires.

The Scriptures, however, speak of deceitful desires (see Ephesians 4:22), evil desires (see James 1:14; 1 Peter 1:14), and sinful desires (see 1 Peter 2:11). It is evil desire that causes us to sin. All sin is desired—or perhaps the perceived benefits of the sin are desired—before it is acted upon. Satan and all other sources of temptation appeal to us first of all through our desires. Eve saw "that the fruit of the tree was good for food and pleasing to the eye, and also desirable for gaining wisdom" (Genesis 3:6). Note how the concept of desire is implied in "good for food" and "pleasing to the eye," as well as explicitly mentioned in "desirable for gaining wisdom."

Mortification then involves a struggle between what we *know* to be right (our convictions) and what we *desire* to do. This is the struggle depicted by the apostle Paul when he wrote, "For the sinful nature desires what is contrary to the Spirit, and the Spirit what is contrary to the sinful nature. They are in conflict with each other, so that you do not do what you want" (Galatians 5:17). The man who has developed a habit of undisciplined and wandering eyes will struggle between a conviction regarding purity and the desire to indulge a lustful look. Whatever our particular areas of vulnerability to sin are, mortification is going to involve struggle—often intense struggle—in those areas.

The ceaselessness of this struggle is suggested to us in Proverbs 27:20: "Death and Destruction are never satisfied, and neither are the eyes of man." Our eyes, of course, are often the gateway to our desires. But whether the appeal to our desires comes through the eye or another avenue such as the memory, our desires are never satisfied. But it is these sinful desires that must be mortified—subdued and weakened in their power to entice us into sin.

It is always emotionally painful to say no to those desires, especially when they represent recurring sin patterns, because those desires run deep and strong. They cry out for fulfillment. That is why Paul used such strong language as "put to death." But if we are going to grow in the area of pursuing holiness, we must learn to mortify our sinful desires.

We cannot do this in the strength of our own willpower, or under the illusion that mortification makes us more acceptable to God. As you seek to pursue holiness—that is, to mortify sin in your life—always keep in mind the "bookends" of Christ's righteousness and Christ's power. Then you will be motivated by gratitude and strengthened by the Holy Spirit as you seek to be holy because God is holy.

CHAPTER 11

THE PRACTICE
OF GODLINESS

I F I HAD to choose one word to summarize all the marks of a mature Christian, it would be the word *godly*. There is no higher compliment that can be paid to a Christian than to call him a godly person. He might be a conscientious parent, a zealous church worker, a dynamic spokesman for Christ, or a talented Christian leader; but none of these things matters if, at the same time, he is not a godly person.

The words *godly* and *godliness* actually appear only a few times in the New Testament; yet the entire Bible is a book on godliness. And when those words do appear they are pregnant with meaning and instruction for us.

When Paul wants to distill the essence of the Christian life into one brief paragraph, he focuses on godliness. He tells us that God's grace "teaches us to say 'No' to *ungodliness* and worldly passions, and to live self-controlled, upright and *godly* lives," as we await the coming of our Lord Jesus Christ (Titus 2:11-13, emphasis added). When Paul thinks of his own job description as an apostle of Jesus Christ, he describes it as being called to further the faith of God's elect and their knowledge of the truth that leads to *godliness* (Titus 1:1).

In his first letter to Timothy, Paul emphasizes godliness. We are to pray for those in authority, that we may live peaceful and quiet lives in all *godliness* and holiness. We are to train ourselves to be *godly*. We are to pursue *godliness*—the word *pursue* indicating unrelenting, persevering effort. *Godliness* with contentment is held forth as great gain; and finally, *godliness* has value for all things, holding promise for both the present life and the life to come.

When Peter, in looking forward to the day of the Lord when the earth and everything in it will be destroyed, asks what kind of people we ought to be, he answers that we are to live holy and *godly* lives (see 2 Peter 3:10-12). Here Peter uses the most momentous event of all history to stir us up to our Christian duty—to live holy and *godly* lives.

Surely, then, godliness is no optional spiritual luxury for a few quaint Christians of a bygone era or for some group of super-saints of today. It is both the privilege and duty of every Christian to pursue godliness, to train himself to be godly, to study diligently the practice of godliness. We don't need any special talent or equipment. God has given to each one of us "everything we need for life and godliness" (2 Peter 1:3). The most ordinary Christian has all that he needs, and the most talented Christian must use those same means in the practice of godliness.

What then is godliness? What are the marks of a godly person? How does a person become godly? I have asked a number of people the question: "What do you think of when you think of godliness?" The answers, though varied, always end up expressing some idea of Christian character, using such expressions as "Godlike," "Christlike," or "the fruit of the Spirit." Godliness certainly includes Christian character, but it is more than that. There is another, even more fundamental aspect of godliness than godly character. It is the foundation, in fact, on which godly character is built.

The New Testament word for godliness, in its original meaning, conveys the idea of a personal attitude toward God that results in actions that are pleasing to God. This personal attitude toward God is what we call devotion to God. But it is always *devotion in action*. It is not just a warm, emotional feeling about God, the kind of feeling we may get while singing some grand old hymn of praise or some contemporary chorus of worship. Neither is devotion to God merely a time of private Bible reading and prayer, a practice we sometimes call "devotions." Although this practice is vitally important to a godly person, we must not think of it as defining devotion to us.

FOCUSED ON GOD

Devotion is not an activity; it is an attitude toward God. God is the focal point of the godly person's life. He or she seeks to practice the presence of God, to enjoy fellowship with God, to do all things to the glory of God, and to see God's name hallowed or honored on earth as it is in heaven.

Being devoted to God doesn't mean a person becomes an ascetic or withdraws from the mundane affairs of ordinary life. It does mean a person goes about the responsibilities of daily life with an eye focused on God. God is never far from his thoughts, and all of his activities are carried out with the aim of pleasing God.

The little-known biblical character of Enoch is an illustration of a godly man. The Bible says little about Enoch, but what it does say helps us understand what godliness is. Genesis 5:22 says Enoch "walked with God." The writer of Hebrews says he "pleased God" (Hebrews 11:5). And in Jude 14-15 he is depicted as deeply concerned about the ungodly society in which he lived.

Enoch is my hero and role model. He was, as far as the biblical record shows, an ordinary man. He was not a leader like Moses, nor a warrior like David, nor an outstanding government official like Daniel. But he was a godly man. He walked with God, and he pleased God. That's what I want to do.

What does it mean to walk with God? According to five commentaries on Genesis that I consulted, it means to have a close, personal communion with God. It means that Enoch spent time focused on God. Enoch did not have the Bible as we have it today, but in whatever manner God communicated Himself to the people of old, Enoch took time to listen. And then he undoubtedly prayed to God. We don't really know how Enoch developed this close, personal relationship with God; but in whatever manner was appropriate for his time, he took advantage of it.

FELLOWSHIP WITH GOD

It is difficult (perhaps impossible?) to live a life focused on God without having a regular time set aside to focus our thoughts on God. Various names are used to describe this focused time. The most popular is the "quiet time." I don't know the history of that term or how it came to be. Perhaps the originator of it thought of quieting our hearts and minds before God so that we can "listen" to Him speak to us through His Word and then speak to Him through our prayers. Or perhaps the person was thinking of the importance of a quiet place or time of day where we can be undisturbed by the activities around us. However it came to be, "quiet time" is the most widely used term to describe this focused time of fellowship with God.

Another term that is used is "devotions" or our "devotional time." This term suggests that the time spent is to be devoted to fellowship with God, again through Bible reading and prayer. There are a number of books with daily Bible readings or meditations or prayers that are called devotional books. The purpose of all of them is to help us focus our minds and hearts on God.

A term that I picked up through a brief acquaintance with a man who is now with the Lord is "fellowship with the Father." I like that because it reminds me that the God whom I want to have fellowship with, the God who is the Creator, Sustainer, and Ruler of the entire universe is, through Jesus Christ, my heavenly Father. He is the One who laid my sins on His Son and gave me His righteousness. He is the One who accepts me unconditionally because I am united to His Son with whom He is well pleased. He is the one to whom I can cry, "*Abba, Father*" (Romans 8:15).

The specific practices of our time of fellowship with the Father vary from person to person. As a minimum, they include some time of Bible reading and prayer. Many people add journaling—a means of writing down thoughts derived from their Bible reading and/or reflections on how God is working in their lives at the time. I like to include a time of private worship (see chapter 14 for more on this subject). One of the most refreshing parts of my fellowship time is what I call "preaching the gospel" to myself. This term I also picked up from the man from whom I learned the term "fellowship with the Father." So it must have been part of his time also. I use a few of a number of gospel Scriptures to "preach to myself." They include Psalm 103:12; Isaiah 53:6; Romans 4:7-8; Romans 8:1; and 2 Corinthians 5:21. This is all part of keeping in place that first "bookend"—Jesus Christ is my righteousness.

The important thing to keep in mind is that this set-aside time, whatever we call it, is to be a time of communion with God. The object is not to read so many chapters of the Bible, though we will read the Bible. Nor is the object to cover all the items on our prayer list, though we will certainly want to pray. The object is to have fellowship with our heavenly Father, whatever activities that may include. I believe I can safely say you cannot be a godly person without a regular focused time of fellowship with God.

———

A LIFE PLEASING TO GOD

Enoch not only walked with God; he also pleased God. Obviously, these are "two sides of a coin." You cannot please God without spending time with Him. At the same time, you cannot have a close, personal communion with God if you are not seeking to please Him. Therefore, I define godliness as *devotion to God that results in a life pleasing to God.* Earlier I said that the devotion to God is always devotion in action. In other words, godliness does imply a godly lifestyle.

So what does a godly lifestyle look like? What is it about some people that causes us to call them godly people? It is their character that reflects this close relationship with God. In the last chapter, "The Pursuit of Holiness," we focused on separating ourselves from sin by mortifying the expressions of sin in our lives. The godly person certainly does this, but he does more than mortify sin. The godly person seeks to put on those positive virtues of Christlike character which Paul calls the fruit of the Spirit (Galatians 5:22-23) and which he elsewhere urges us to "clothe" ourselves with (Colossians 3:12-14).

There is some duplication in these two lists; and when the duplications are eliminated, you have twelve different positive character traits we should seek to put on: love, joy, peace, patience, kindness, goodness, faithfulness, gentleness, self-control, compassion, humility, and a forgiving spirit.

Obviously, an individual treatment of each of these godly character traits is beyond the scope of this book. I have addressed most of them in my book, *The Practice of Godliness*. I do want to cover briefly the two traits I believe are fundamental to all the rest: love and humility. Love is undoubtedly the most fundamental character trait. In fact, it is taught, either by precept or example, more than fifty times in the New Testament.

======

THE GRACE OF LOVE

When Paul lists the godly traits he calls the fruit of the Spirit, he puts love first—very likely to emphasize its importance. Love is the overall grace from which all the others grow. In Colossians 3:14, he says love binds all the other virtues together in perfect unity.

Godliness is devotion to God, but devotion to God finds its outward expression in loving one another. Or, to state it another way, our devotion to God is validated by our love for other people. As the apostle John puts it, "For anyone who does not love his brother, whom he has seen, cannot love God, whom he has not seen. And he has given us this command: Whoever loves God must also love his brother" (1 John 4:20-21).

We cannot truly love God without loving one another. To recognize that there is someone I do not love is to say to God, "I do not love you enough to love that person." This is not to deny the reality of spiritual struggle in loving a particular person, because it often exists. I am referring to the attitude of not even wanting to love the person, of being content to allow a lack of love for someone to reside in my heart unchecked and unchallenged.

Devotion to God is the ultimate motivation for Christian character, but it is also true that love for our brother is the more proximate motivation for the exercise of Christian graces among one another.

First Corinthians 13 is the classic description of love. If we rephrased the virtues of love in 1 Corinthians 13 in terms of motivational statements, they might sound something like this:

- I am patient with you because I love you and want to forgive you.
- I am kind to you because I love you and want to help you.
- I do not envy your possessions or your gifts because I love you and want you to have the best.
- I do not boast about my attainments because I love you and want to hear about yours.
- I am not proud because I love you and want to esteem you before myself.
- I am not rude because I love you and care about your feelings.
- I am not self-seeking because I love you and want to meet your needs.
- I am not easily angered by you because I love you and want to overlook your offenses.
- I do not keep a record of your wrongs because I love you, and "love covers a multitude of sins."

Expressing love in this manner, as a motivational factor, helps us see what Paul had in mind when he said that love binds together all the virtues of Christian character. Love is not so much a character trait as the inner disposition of the soul that produces them all. But although love may be more a motivational force than an actual display of Christian virtue, it *always* results in actions on our part. Love inclines us and directs us to be kind, to forgive, to give of ourselves to one another. Therefore, Peter says to us, "Above all, love each other deeply" (1 Peter 4:8).

THE GRACE OF HUMILITY

I believe the second most important character trait is humility. Again, I address that trait briefly in my book, *Transforming Grace,* chapter 13, "Garments of Grace." I like to use the term, *gospel humility,* because I believe a thorough understanding of our need for the gospel and our daily appropriation of it is the primary instrument God uses to produce humility in us. Who can be proud kneeling at the foot of the cross? It is when we turn our eyes away from the cross and try to build our own track record of works-righteousness that we begin to exhibit self-righteousness and pride instead of gospel humility.

A person living by the gospel will seek to clothe himself with *humility.* Unfortunately this particular fruit of the Spirit is not eagerly sought after by most believers. Perhaps that is because it is often confused with self-depreciation, which denies there is any good or worth in us. Humility does not deny the good in us. Rather it recognizes that the good in us in the form of Christlike character, and the good done by us in service to God and other people, is totally undeserved on our part and is due to the work of the Holy Spirit in our lives. But humility does not deny the evidences of His gracious work in us and through us. To do so would be to dishonor Him as much as to ascribe the cause and results of His working to ourselves.

Jesus not only said, "No branch can bear fruit by itself," but He also said, "If a man remains in me and I in him, he will bear much fruit" (John 15:4-5). To remain, or to use words we are more familiar with, to abide in Christ is to set aside our own wisdom, strength, and merit in order to draw all from Him. In other words, to abide in Christ is the same as to depend totally on God's grace, both in the realm of ability and in the realm of merit. But the point I want to make here is

Jesus did say that when we abide in Him, when we depend on the grace of God, we will bear much fruit. So it is not honoring to God, nor is it a mark of true humility to refuse to see the good produced in us or through us. Humility, then, is a recognition that we are at the same time completely weak and helpless in ourselves, but powerful and useful by the grace of God.

There is also the horizontal dimension of humility in relationship to other people. Pride, in relation to other people, is comparing ourselves with others and seeing ourselves as superior to them in some way—whether it be in character, conduct, or achievement. One of the worst forms of pride is spiritual pride—an attitude that I am more holy, or righteous, or faithful, or obedient, or more fruitful in evangelism than others.

Humility toward others, then, is once again a recognition that all we are and do that is of any worth is a gift of God's grace. Hence, humility turns the temptation to pride into an occasion for gratitude to God for what He has done in and through us.

There is another aspect of humility in relation to other people—that of service to others. Paul probably had this aspect in mind when he said in Colossians 3:12 that we should clothe ourselves with humility. Jesus was our example in serving. He washed His disciples' feet—the usual task of the most lowly servant—and told His disciples they should follow His example (see John 13:1-15). He said, "For who is greater, the one who is at the table or the one who serves? Is it not the one who is at the table? But I am among you as one who serves" (Luke 22:27). Above all, Jesus laid aside His glory and became the ultimate servant, dying for us on the cross (see Philippians 2:5-11). By His actions, Jesus turned what was deemed a weakness by pagans into a strength and virtue for Christians. The person who wants to be godly must clothe himself with humility by serving others.

=====

PRACTICE, PRACTICE, PRACTICE

I have titled this chapter "The Practice of Godliness," which is also the title of my book on the subject. Why the *practice* of godliness? Two reasons: First, developing godly character does require work. Paul wrote to Timothy, ". . . *train* [that is work at it] yourself to be godly" (1 Timothy 4:7). Second, we will never attain perfect godliness in this life. Just as we will never be completely holy, so we will never be completely godly until we go to be with Jesus. Just as we should always pursue holiness, so we should constantly be practicing godliness. The key to attaining and maintaining any skill is practice, practice, practice. And this is true of our growth in godliness.

CHAPTER 12

TRUSTING GOD

ALL OF US face adversity in various forms and at different times. As someone has said so well, "Life is difficult." I would go further. I would say life is often painful. Life often hurts. Nothing I say in this chapter is intended to make light of our pain. I simply want to help us learn to trust God in the midst of it.

Some adversities are fairly minimal. I left my Bible on an airplane just two hours before a speaking engagement. That's not exactly traumatic, but it seemed like it at the time. Some adversities are sudden and devastating, such as an auto accident that kills one or more loved ones. Others are chronic and persistent, such as an incurable physical disability. Even when we aren't experiencing major heartaches, we often encounter those frustrating or anxiety-producing events, such as the loss of my Bible, that can rob us of our peace and joy.

A major part of spiritual growth is learning to trust God in such times of adversity. It is just as important to trust God as it is to obey Him. When we disobey God, we defy His authority and despise His holiness. But when we don't trust God, we doubt His sovereignty and question His goodness. In both cases, we cast aspersions upon His character.

Yet it often seems more difficult to trust God than to obey Him. The moral will of God is rational and reasonable. The circumstances in which we must trust God often appear irrational and inexplicable. Obeying God is worked out in well-defined boundaries of His revealed will. Trusting God is worked out in an arena that has no boundaries. As Proverbs 27:1 says we "do not know what a day may bring forth."

In order to trust God, we must always view our adverse circumstances through the eyes of faith, not of sense. And just as the faith of salvation comes through hearing the message of the gospel (see Romans 10:17), so the faith to trust God in adversity comes through the Word of God alone. It is only in the Scriptures that we find an adequate view of God's relationship to and involvement in our painful circumstances. It is only from the Scriptures applied to our hearts by the Holy Spirit that we receive the grace to trust God in adversity.

In the arena of adversity, the Scriptures teach us three essential truths about God—truths we must believe if we are to trust Him in adversity. They are:

- God is completely sovereign.
- God is infinite in wisdom.
- God is perfect in love.

BOTH SOVEREIGN AND GOOD

The Bible continually asserts the sovereignty of God, and yet today many people, including some Christians, question it. They reason this way: God is either sovereign and not good or else He is good and not sovereign. If He were both, we would not experience and see all the heartache and tragedy that occurs daily around the world.

142

Having decided God cannot be both sovereign and good, they choose to believe in the goodness or love of God. But Jesus said we don't have to choose between God's sovereignty and His goodness. Consider what He says about God's involvement in the destiny of a sparrow:

> Are not two sparrows sold for a penny? Yet not one
> of them will fall to the ground apart from the will of
> your Father. And even the very hairs of your head are
> all numbered. So don't be afraid; you are worth more
> than many sparrows. (Matthew 10:29-31)

A sparrow cannot fall to the ground apart from God's sovereign will. Regardless of how many hunters or birds of prey are after that sparrow, nothing can happen to it unless God so wills it. And then Jesus does not leave us in doubt as to His application for us. He said, "So don't be afraid; you are worth more than many sparrows."

In effect, Jesus is saying, "If God sovereignly controls the destiny of a sparrow, how much more does He control your destiny? Therefore, don't be afraid."

Someone may say, "Well, it's well and good God controls the destiny of a sparrow. But what about major calamities such as the AIDS epidemic and the vast areas of famine in Africa? Is God sovereign over the major tragedies of the world?"

The Bible says yes. Over and over again, the Bible asserts the sovereignty of God over both the minutiae and the major events of life. Here is just one example from Lamentations 3:37-38: "Who can speak and have it happen if the Lord has not decreed it? Is it not from the mouth of the Most High that both calamities and good things come?"

This passage teaches us that neither human beings nor the impersonal forces of nature nor other physical circumstances can harm us unless God decrees it. God may decree to cause an event positively, or He may decree to allow it. But in either case, He is sovereign over it.

So we see that God is sovereign. But what about His goodness? Consider again the words of Jesus in Luke 12:6-7: "Are not five sparrows sold for two pennies? Yet not one of them is forgotten by God. Indeed, the very hairs of your head are all numbered. Don't be afraid; you are worth more than many sparrows."

Do you see the subtle difference between this Scripture and Matthew 10:29-31? There, Jesus speaks of the sovereignty of God. Here, in Luke, He speaks about the care of God. Not a single sparrow is forgotten by Him. The word *forgotten* here does not refer to a lapse of memory on God's part. Rather, Jesus is saying not a single sparrow is abandoned by God. Once again, Jesus does not leave us in doubt as to His application. If a single sparrow is not forgotten by God, how much more does He not forget you?

The reality of life, though, is that it often seems that God has forgotten or abandoned us. In Psalm 13:1, David cries out "How long, O LORD? Will you forget me forever? How long will you hide your face from me?" And in Psalm 10:1, he prays, "Why, O LORD, do you stand far off? Why do you hide yourself in times of trouble?" It's as if David is saying, "God, just when I need You most, I can't find You. You've hidden Yourself."

We find a similar heart cry from the nation of Israel [called Zion in the text] in Isaiah 49:14-16: "But Zion said, 'The LORD has forsaken me, the Lord has forgotten me.' Can a mother forget the baby at her breast and have no compassion on the child she has borne? Though she may forget, I will not forget you! See, I have engraved you on the palms of my hands; your walls are ever before me."

The two words, *forsaken* and *forgotten,* refer to a heart forsakenness and a physical abandonment. This is what happens in the unbelievably cruel practice of infanticide. In biblical times, unwanted babies were left out in the open field to be eaten by animals or die of exposure. They were physically abandoned. But, obviously, for parents to do such a horrible thing, they first had to forsake the baby in their hearts. This is what Zion accuses God of doing.

But what is God's answer? He takes the closest physical bond there is—that of a mother nursing her baby—and asks, "Can this mother abandon this child?" Then God says, "Though she may forget, I will not forget you." God says it is impossible for Him to forget us even though our circumstances may make it appear to the contrary sometimes.

So what do we do when it seems as if God has forgotten and forsaken us? We go back to what the Bible tells us about God. We can look at God through the lens of our pain, or we can look at our pain through the lens of faith. And faith always comes through reliance on the promises of God. This is where Psalm 119:11 can help us. We can store up God's promises in our hearts against the time when we face adversity, whether large or small. I can't tell you how many times I've had to call to mind the words of Hebrews 13:5, "Never will I leave you; never will I forsake you," in my own circumstances.

―――――

THE WISDOM OF GOD

We see then that God is both sovereign and good. We don't have to choose between them. But the question still remains. If God is both sovereign and good, why is there so much heartache and tragedy in the world? Why doesn't God restrain both the moral and circumstantial evil in the world? The answer is: We don't know but God does. And God has no obligation to explain it to us. In fact, we probably couldn't understand if He did explain. Consider the words of Paul in

Romans 11:33: "How unsearchable his judgments, and his paths beyond tracing out!" Or as one translation expresses that last phrase: ". . . how mysterious his methods."

Suppose a prominent physicist is explaining some intricate nuclear equation to a seminar of his peers. He has it all written out on a whiteboard and is going through the equation. His peers can follow his logic, but a six-year-old couldn't. The scientist could explain it over and over again, but the six-year-old simply doesn't have the intellectual capacity to understand.

This is the way we are in relation to God's wisdom, only more so. The gap in understanding between the physicist and the six-year-old is huge. But it is still finite. But the gap between God's ways of governing His universe and our ability to track His ways is an infinite gap. As God Himself says,

> "For my thoughts are not your thoughts, neither are your ways my ways," declares the LORD. "As the heavens are higher than the earth, so are my ways higher than your ways and my thoughts than your thoughts." (Isaiah 55:8-9)

Now the expression, "higher than the heavens," may not be so striking to us in the space age. But remember: God spoke those words hundreds of years before the Wright brothers flew their first airplane. At that time, "higher than the heavens" would have been a metaphor for infinity. That's the way God's ways are to our ways. They are infinitely above them.

So, if we are going to learn to trust God, we must accept the fact that we have to trust Him when we don't understand. But remember: Although we don't understand His ways, we know they are good.

Remember the three truths that the Bible teaches us about God and our adversities:

- God is completely sovereign.
- God is infinite in wisdom.
- God is perfect in love.

Someone has expressed these three truths, as they relate to us, in this way:

God in His love always wills what is best for us. In His wisdom, He always knows what is best. And in His sovereignty, He has the power to bring it about.

======

THE DISCIPLINE OF ADVERSITY

Although we may not be able to understand the way God governs His universe or why He allows specific instances of pain in our individual lives, He has given us an idea of the ultimate purpose for the adversities we face. In Hebrews 12:5-11, he calls it *discipline*. As used in that passage, discipline does not refer to remedial punishment, as in "I had to discipline my son." Rather, the word has the idea of child-training—all that which goes into training a child to be a responsible adult.

In Hebrews 12, the writer uses *discipline* to refer to a specific aspect of God's spiritual child-training—that of hardship or adversity.

Hebrews 12:7 is key to understanding the purpose of adversity in our lives. The writer says, "Endure hardship as discipline." There is no qualifying adjective. He did not say, "Endure all hardship"; neither did he say, "Endure some hardship as discipline." In the absence of a qualifying adjective, we must understand him to have meant all hardship.

147

All hardship of whatever kind has a disciplinary purpose for us. *There is no such thing as pain without a purpose in the life of a believer.*

This does not necessarily mean a particular hardship is related to a specific act or habit of sin in our lives. It does mean every expression of discipline has as its intended end conformity to the likeness of Christ. It is true we often cannot see the connection between the adversity and God's purpose. It should be enough for us, however, to know God sees the connection and the end result He intends.

Can we tell if a particular adversity is related to some specific sin in our lives? Not with certainty, but it is my own belief the Holy Spirit will bring such a connection to our attention if we need to know in order to deal with a particular sin. If nothing comes to mind, we can pray, asking God if there is something He wants us to consciously learn. Beyond that, however, it is vain to speculate as to why God has brought a particular hardship into our lives. Part of the sanctifying process of adversity is its mystery or our inability to make any sense out of a particular hardship.

When we are unable to make any sense of our circumstances, we need to come back to the assurance in Hebrews 12:7 — "God is treating you as sons." Remember, He is the one in charge of our spiritual growth. He knows exactly what and how much adversity will develop more Christlikeness in us, and He will not bring, nor allow to come into our lives, any more than is needful for His purpose.

Endure all hardship as discipline. I don't want to trivialize hardship, but as I have already acknowledged, there are varying degrees of adversity. Some are life-shattering, such as the death of a loved one or a permanently disabling injury. Some, such as a flat tire or a stopped-up sink, are really only temporary nuisances. But, whether trivial or serious, all of these circumstances and events are intended by God to be means of developing more Christlike character.

SUBMISSION TO DISCIPLINE

Continuing in his treatment of the discipline of adversity, the author of Hebrews wrote, "Moreover, we have all had human fathers who disciplined us and we respected them for it. How much more should we submit to the Father of our spirits and live!" (Hebrews 12:9).

In order to gain the most profit from the discipline of hardship, we need to submit to it. The writer reminds us that in the human family, the children respect the father who disciplines them. This, of course, may be difficult to see in families where the father disciplines for selfish reasons—out of anger and impatience—instead of out of love for the benefit of the child. In his analogy between human parental discipline and God's discipline, however, the writer of Hebrews assumes a more normal father model.

The writer's point is that if we respected our fathers' discipline, how much more should we submit to God's discipline? Our fathers' discipline was at best imperfect, both in motive and in application. But God's discipline is perfect, exactly suited to our needs.

How then do we submit to God's discipline? Negatively, it means that we do not become angry at God, or charge Him with injustice, when very difficult circumstances come into our lives. I was prone to write, "do not remain angry," instead of, "do not become angry at God," to allow for an initial short-term reaction toward God. But I believe even short-term anger toward God is sin for which we need to repent. Even though the anger may be an emotional response, it is still a charge of injustice against God. Surely that is sin.

It is even more serious, however, when someone allows anger toward God to continue over months or even years. Such an attitude amounts to a grudge against God and is actually rebellion. It is certainly not submitting to our heavenly Father.

Positively, we submit to God's discipline when we accept all hardship as coming from His loving hand for our good. This means that our primary response would be one of humble submission and trust. As the apostle Peter wrote, "Humble yourselves, therefore, under God's mighty hand, that he may lift you up in due time" (1 Peter 5:6). We should submit to God's providential dealings with us, knowing there is still much in our characters that needs improving. We should trust Him, believing He is infinite in His wisdom and knows exactly the kind and extent of adversity we need to accomplish His purpose.

Submitting to God's discipline doesn't mean we should not pray for relief from the difficulty or should not seek legitimate means to gain relief. Sometimes the end God has in mind is to exercise our faith, so He brings us into straitened circumstances so that we might look up to Him and see His deliverance. But strengthening our faith is an important aspect of discipline.

The main thing is our attitude. We can pray earnestly to God for relief and still be submissive to Him regarding the outcome. Jesus is our supreme example in this as He prayed the night before His crucifixion, "My Father, if it is possible, may this cup be taken from me. Yet not as I will, but as you will" (Matthew 26:39).

THE GOAL OF ADVERSITY

Our fathers disciplined us for a little while as they thought best; but God disciplines us for our good, that we may share in his holiness. No discipline seems pleasant at the time, but painful. Later on,

however, it produces a harvest of righteousness
and peace for those who have been trained by it.
(Hebrews 12:10-11)

The writer of Hebrews contrasts the finite wisdom of human parents in disciplining children with the infinite, infallible wisdom of God. Even the best human parents can only discipline as they think best. Their judgment is fallible; their actions are sometimes inconsistent and are often guided by the impulse of the moment. As is often observed, they have to learn by doing. Anyone who has tried to rear children in a godly, responsible manner knows there are times when parents simply do not know what is the appropriate manner or degree of discipline for a child.

God, however, always disciplines us for our good. He knows what is best for each one of us. He doesn't have to debate with Himself over what is most suitable for us. He knows intuitively and perfectly the nature, intensity, and duration of adversity that will best serve His purpose to make us partakers of His holiness. He never brings more pain than is needed to accomplish His purpose. Lamentations 3:33 expresses that sentiment this way: "For he does not willingly bring affliction or grief to the children of men."

Returning to Hebrews 12:10—"God disciplines us for our good, that we may share in his holiness." Observe how the writer equated our good with becoming more holy. The apostle Paul wrote in a similar manner when he said, "And we know that in all things God works for the good of those who love him. . . . For those God foreknew he also predestined to be conformed to the likeness of his Son" (Romans 8:28-29). To be conformed to the likeness of Christ and to share in God's holiness are equivalent expressions. That is the highest good to which the believer can aspire.

This is the design of God in all of the adversity and heartache we experience in this life. From God's perspective, there is no such thing as random or chance events in our lives. All pain we experience is intended to move us closer to the goal of being holy as He is holy.

"No discipline seems pleasant at the time," the writer to the Hebrews said. Adversity comes in many forms: serious illness or injury, death of a loved one, unemployment, disappointments, and humiliations of various kinds. All of these afflictions are painful. They have to be to accomplish their intended purpose of pruning away what is unholy in our lives so that true holy character may be produced. We should admit the pain. We should be like the writer of Hebrews who was honest when he said the discipline of hardship is painful.

Later on, however, the discipline produces a harvest of righteousness and peace. The "harvest of righteousness" is essentially equivalent to sharing in His holiness. Discipline, then, is one of the chief means God uses to make us holy. The road to holiness is paved with adversity. If we want to be holy, we must expect the discipline of God through the heartaches and disappointments He brings or allows to come into our lives.

The discipline of hardship also produces peace for those who have been trained by it. The word trained used here is the same one Paul used in 1 Timothy 4:7, which he borrowed from the athletic world of that day. It is not clear whether the author of Hebrews was writing of the peace that comes with maturity in this life or the rest that comes ultimately to the believer in eternity. The truth is, both are taught in Scripture. Concerning this life, Paul wrote that our sufferings produce perseverance, which in turn produces character (see Romans 5:3-4), and James said that the testing of our faith develops perseverance, which leads to maturity (see James 1:2-4).

Our ultimate hope, though, is not in maturity of character in this life, as valuable as that is, but in the perfection of character in eternity. The apostle John wrote, "When he appears, we shall be like him, for we shall see him as he is" (1 John 3:2). The often-painful process of being transformed into His likeness will be over. We shall be completely conformed to the likeness of the Lord Jesus Christ.

Looking forward to that time, Paul wrote, "I consider that our present sufferings are not worth comparing with the glory that will be revealed in us" (Romans 8:18). Paul said our sufferings are not worth comparing with the glory we will experience in eternity.

This is not to say our present hardships are not painful. We have already seen from Hebrews 12:11 that they are indeed painful, and we all know this to some degree from experience. Nothing I say in this chapter is intended to minimize the pain and perplexity of adversity. But we need to learn to look by faith beyond the present pain to the eternal glory that will be revealed in us. Remember, the God who disciplines us will also glorify us.

So the discipline of adversity is given to us by God as a means of our growth. Our role in this discipline is to respond to it and to acquiesce to whatever God may be doing, even though a particular instance of adversity makes no sense to us. As we do this, we will see in due time the fruit of the Spirit produced in our lives. We will grow more and more into the believers God wants us to be.

CHAPTER 13

SERVING GOD

THE GOAL OF our spiritual growth is to become more and more like Jesus (see Romans 8:29). We tend to think of this as becoming more like Him in His character, but we need to remember that Jesus came to *work*—to *do* the will of the Father. On the eve of His crucifixion, He could say in His prayer, "I have brought you glory on earth by completing the work you gave me to do" (John 17:4).

So, if we are going to become like Jesus, we also must do the work God has given us to do. In fact, Paul tells us in Ephesians 2:10 that "we are God's workmanship, created in Christ Jesus to do good works, which God prepared in advance for us to do." God intends for all believers to be active workers in His kingdom.

To this end God has assigned every Christian a function in the body of Christ. There are no exceptions to this; every member has a function to fulfill. Warren Myers, in his book, *Pray: How to Be Effective in Prayer,* tells of two remarkable people: William Carey, missionary to India, and Carey's bedridden, almost totally paralyzed sister. William Carey accomplished a Bible translation work unequaled in missionary history and has been called "the father of modern missions." We don't even know his sister's name. She is mentioned only as Carey's sister. But while Carey labored in India translating and printing parts or all of the Bible into forty languages, his sister lay on her back in London and prayed hour after hour, month after month, for all the details, problems, and struggles of her brother's work. In telling this story of Carey and his sister, Myers asks the question, "To whose account will God credit the victories won through this remarkable man?"[1] We all know that Carey's sister shared in his ministry. In fact, she was a very vital part. Without her ministry of intercession on her brother's behalf, the work would not have gone forward.

FUNCTION IN THE BODY

The point of this story is to emphasize that God assigns to *every* believer an important function in the body. He assigned William Carey to do Bible translation work in India, and He assigned his sister to pray for that work as she lay paralyzed in her bed in London. William Carey's function was highly visible, at least it is to us today; his sister's function was probably unknown except to a few people. Yet both had a vital part to play in the missionary enterprise in India. God assigned each of them a specific function and enabled them by His grace to fulfill it.

Just as God assigns to each of us a function in the body of Christ, so He equips each of us to fulfill that function. In the New Testament this equipping is called a "gift." *A spiritual gift is an ability given by God and empowered by the Holy Spirit to perform the specific function within the body that God has assigned to each of us.* Spiritual gifts are distinct from natural abilities, although the gifts frequently incorporate some natural ability. While both gifts and abilities are endowments from God, gifts are related specifically to the function God has assigned to us in the body.

In his discourse on spiritual gifts in Romans 12:3-8, Paul, using the analogy of the physical body, said, "Just as each of us has one body with many members, and these members do not all have the same function, so in Christ we who are many form one body. . . . We have different gifts, according to the grace given us" (verses 4-6). Note the relationship between function and gift. We all have different functions and, consequently, different gifts that enable us to fulfill those functions.

Our gifts are always consistent with our functions. If we view the church of Jesus Christ as His *body,* then we recognize that we are members of that body, sharing together a common life in Christ and using our spiritual gifts to serve one another, mutually building each other up in the faith. If we view the church as a spiritual enterprise engaged in carrying out Christ's Great Commission to make disciples in all nations, then we have been called by God to be a team of dedicated partners actively involved in that effort. Whether it's building up the body of Christ or reaching out to those without Christ, each of us has a function to fulfill, and we have received the necessary gifting to fulfill it.

PRINCIPLES OF SPIRITUAL GIFTS

Having seen that all of us have a function in the body and the corresponding gifts to fulfill it, we need to consider certain basic truths or principles regarding spiritual gifts.

(1) *The purpose of all spiritual gifts is to serve others and to glorify God.* Consider 1 Peter 4:10, along with verse 11: "Each one should use whatever gift he has received to serve others. . . . so that in all things God may be praised through Jesus Christ." According to Peter, there are two objectives in the use of our gifts: serving others and glorifying or praising God. He also referred to us as stewards in the use of our gifts:

"Use [your gift] to serve one another, as good stewards of God's varied grace" (1 Peter 4:10, ESV). When used in this sense, "steward" refers to a person who manages someone else's property, finances, or other affairs. Our gifts are not our property to use as we please; they are a trust committed to us by God to use for others and for His glory as He directs.

There is no place in the use of spiritual gifts for the seeking of recognition, fame, or self-fulfillment. Some gifts by their nature are more public than others, and thus they are more prone to result in recognition. This would be true, for example, of the gifts of teaching and music. These people exercise their gifts "up front." Everyone knows who they are. There are others who exercise the gift of service in seeing that the physical aspects of a church or campus ministry setting are in place and properly functioning. Hardly anyone ever sees the work they do. In fact, as long as they do their job properly, few people even think about it; their work is taken for granted by most people.

As long as we keep in mind the purpose of gifts, however, we will not be concerned about recognition or fame. We will seek to use our gifts as stewards entrusted with the grace of God to be used to serve others and to glorify Him. Whether ours is a public gift like teaching or a less noticeable gift like serving, the end objective is "that in all things God may be praised through Jesus Christ."

(2) *Every Christian has a gift and every gift is important.* As has already been stated, God has assigned every believer a function in the body of Christ and has consequently gifted every member to fulfill that function. We need to underscore this point. God has given a spiritual gift to every individual believer in the body of Christ. Paul expressly says, "Now to each one the manifestation of the Spirit is given for the common good" (1 Corinthians 12:7). It is important we acknowledge this fact because so many Christians seem to have the attitude that they do not have a gift.

Not only do we each have a gift, each one of our gifts is important. Again we tend to recognize the more public, noticeable gifts as important and the low profile gifts as perhaps not so important. The apostle Paul anticipates this tendency when he envisions the foot saying, "Because I am not a hand, I do not belong to the body," and the ear saying, "Because I am not an eye, I do not belong to the body" (1 Corinthians 12:15-16). Here Paul has in mind the person with the less noticeable gift comparing himself with the person with the more noticeable gift and then feeling that he has no gift at all.

Of course there is also a danger that those with the more public gifts will secretly disregard or belittle the contribution to the body of those who have the less noticeable gifts. Again Paul anticipates this tendency in 1 Corinthians 12:21 when he says, "The eye cannot say to the hand, 'I don't need you!' And the head cannot say to the feet, 'I don't need you!'" We all need each other's contribution in the body. Just as some functions in the human body are in a sense more important than others, so it is with some gifts in the body of Christ. Paul seems to recognize this in verses 28-31 of 1 Corinthians 12. But this does not change the fact that *all* gifts are important. Some may be more important than others, perhaps, but none are unimportant. So whether we have the less important or the more important gifts, let us not envy the one or despise the other. We need to recognize each gift is necessary in the body and is important to God.

(3) *Gifts are sovereignly bestowed by God.* Just as God assigns us certain functions in the body, so He bestows our gifts. Speaking of gifts in 1 Corinthians 12:11, Paul says, "All these are the work of one and the same Spirit, and he gives them to each one, just as he determines." Again using the physical body as an analogy, Paul states in verse 18, "God has arranged the parts in the body, every one of them, just as he wanted them to be." The obvious inference is that just as God sovereignly

arranged the parts of the physical body, so He sovereignly arranged us as individual parts in the body of Christ.

Perhaps this principle seems too obvious to state, but consider the implications and the applications of it. You possess the gifts you have because the sovereign God of the universe wanted you to be that way. He ordained a plan for your life before you were even born, and He has gifted you specifically to carry out that plan. Never disparage your gift. If you do, you are disparaging the plan of God and perhaps complaining against Him. Similarly, never look down on the gift of another. If you do, you are scorning the plan of God for that person.

God not only determines what gift (or gifts[2]) each of us has; He also determines the measure or extent of that gift. Two people may have the same gift but in different measure. Consider two teachers of the Word equally gifted—one laboring in obscurity and the other enjoying widespread recognition. Why the difference? I believe the usual explanation is that the two people are gifted in the same area, but one is more gifted than the other. Both gifts are being carried out under the sovereign providence of God.

Jesus spoke of three servants receiving different amounts of "talents," each according to his ability (see Matthew 25:14-30). A biblical "talent" was not a mental or physical ability but an amount of money, something more than a thousand dollars. Each of the servants was to invest a certain sum of money in order to earn interest. Apparently each servant had the same calling to invest money. But they had different degrees of ability within that calling, and so they received different degrees of responsibility according to their abilities.

It is the same way with spiritual gifts. God gives us not only the particular gift we have, but also the measure of that gift. Then He holds us responsible to use our gift to its full measure. The person who has a greater measure of a certain gift has greater responsibility for it.

"From everyone who has been given much, much will be demanded" (Luke 12:48). The three servants in the parable of the talents were judged not in relation to each other but according to how they used what had been entrusted to them.

(4) *Every gift is given by God's grace.* The Greek word for a spiritual gift is *charisma,* which means "a gift of God's grace," whether it is the gift of eternal life as in Romans 6:23 or the gift of a spiritual ability for use in the body. Paul said, "We have different gifts, according to the *grace* given us," and Peter said, "Each one should use whatever gift he has received to serve others, faithfully administering God's *grace* in its various forms" (Romans 12:6, 1 Peter 4:10, emphasis added). None of us deserves the gift we have been given. All the gifts are given by God's undeserved favor to us through Christ.

In Ephesians 3:7-8, Paul testified freely that he did not deserve to be an apostle of Jesus Christ:

> I became a servant of this gospel by the gift of God's
> grace given me through the working of his power.
> Although I am less than the least of all God's people,
> this grace was given me: to preach to the Gentiles the
> unsearchable riches of Christ.

According to this principle, the most worthy and the most unworthy of all Christians both receive their gifts on the same basis. The unworthy person surely does not deserve his gift, but neither does the most worthy. They both receive them as unmerited favors from God. The highly gifted person should not think he is so gifted because of his hard work or his faithfulness in previous service to God. Likewise, the person who feels he has wasted a good part of his life and is consequently undeserving of any spiritual gift should not despair. Paul said he received his gift despite the fact that he was the least of all God's people. Worthy or unworthy, it makes no difference. All gifts are given by God's grace.

(5) *All gifts must be developed and exercised.* Even though gifts are given by God's grace, it is our responsibility to develop and exercise them. Paul exhorted Timothy to rekindle or "fan into flame the gift of God," and elsewhere Paul told him, "Do not neglect your gift" (2 Timothy 1:6, 1 Timothy 4:14).

In order to exercise our spiritual gifts effectively, even though they are sovereignly and graciously bestowed, we must develop and use them. The effective use of our gifts does not occur without diligent effort on our part. Timothy already had the gift of teaching, yet Paul did not hesitate to urge him to be diligent to present himself to God as a workman who could correctly handle the Word of Truth. And in 1 Timothy, after exhorting Timothy not to neglect his gift, Paul said, "Be diligent in these matters; give yourself wholly to them" (1 Timothy 4:15). Timothy's use of his gift was not a matter of indifference. He was accountable to God for his development and use of it.

This means hard work. The person with the gift of teaching must study zealously to learn God's truth and must then labor diligently to communicate it in a clear and inspiring manner. The person with the gift of service must strive to become competent and proficient in his particular area of service in order to ensure that the results of his labors reflect a standard of excellence that glorifies God. There is no place for either shoddy teaching or shoddy service in God's kingdom.

The believer with the gift of mercy must study how to use that gift in a way that best relieves the sufferings and miseries of others. The person who has the gift of leadership must study the principles of leadership in order to use his gift most effectively, and then, as Paul said, he must govern diligently. Simply having a spiritual gift does not mean we can automatically fulfill our function in the body without diligent effort.

Rather, we are responsible to develop and use the gifts God has given us.

(6) *The effective use of every gift is dependent on faith in Christ.* Although gifts are sovereignly bestowed and their effective exercise involves hard work and diligent effort, it is also true no gift is exercised apart from faith in Christ. We cannot assume God's blessing on our efforts even though we are laboring within the bounds of the gifts He has given us. The necessity of conscious dependence on Christ for His enabling power is a fundamental fact for every aspect of the Christian life, whether in spiritual growth in our own lives or in service within the body. "Apart from me," Jesus said, "you can do nothing" (John 15:5).

Speaking of his own diligent efforts, Paul wrote to the believers at Colosse, "To this end I labor, struggling with all [Christ's] energy, which so powerfully works in me" (Colossians 1:29). Paul labored diligently in the exercising of his gifts. In fact, as we have already seen, he described his labor as "struggling." Yet he also relied on Christ. The persevering apostle struggled with the energy that Christ infused in him as he labored in dependence on Him.

To maintain the proper perspective of diligent personal responsibility and a sincere attitude of total dependence on Christ for His power requires constant vigilance in two directions. On the one hand, we can be guilty of slothfulness in the development or use of our gifts under the pretext that we are "trusting in the Lord." On the other hand, we can presume on God's blessing as we attempt to use our gifts in the strength of our own abilities or in the fact that we have "done that so many times."

(7) *Only love will give true value to our gifts.* In any discussion of spiritual gifts we should give careful attention to the fact that the classic Scripture passage on Christian love, 1 Corinthians 13, is set right in the middle of the Bible's most extensive treatment on spiritual gifts. We have already looked briefly at 1 Corinthians 13 in chapter 11, but here

I want us to look at it in relation to the exercise of our gifts. In the first part of chapter 13, Paul tells us that even if we possess the greatest of gifts, have the most extraordinary faith, and display an amazing amount of zeal and courage yet have not love, we are nothing and we accomplish nothing.

It is not that Paul sets love over spiritual gifts or Christian zeal as if love is more important than gifts, faith, or zeal. Rather, he says it is love that gives all these other areas value and worth. The gifts and character traits Paul mentions in 1 Corinthians 13:1-3 are not insignificant or commonplace. Whatever we may think about the bestowal and use of some of these gifts today, the fact is that in Paul's day the gifts of tongues and prophecy were the most coveted of gifts. And who of us would not desire the faith that can move mountains or the sacrificial spirit that would prompt us to give our goods to the poor or the spiritual courage that enables martyrs to endure the flames?

Yet Paul very plainly said, not once but three times, that only love gives value to our gifts, our faith, and our zeal. If we set our hearts only on the exercising of our gifts, the increase of our faith, and the promotion of our zeal and courage, without seeking to grow in love, we will be as nothing and accomplish nothing. We may generate a lot of Christian activity, gain some measure of fame, and even appear to accomplish something for God. But if we have not love, it all amounts to nothing.

Write down, either in your imagination or on a sheet of paper, a row of zeros. Keep adding zeros until you have filled a whole line on the page. What do they add up to? Exactly nothing! Even if you were to write a thousand of them, they would still be nothing. But put a positive number in front of them and immediately they have value. This is the way it is with our gifts and faith and zeal. They are the zeros on the page. Without love, they count for nothing. But put love in front of them and immediately they have value.[3] And just as the number two gives more value to a row of zeros than the number one does, so more and more love can add exponentially greater value to our gifts.

Notice how Paul describes love in 1 Corinthians 13:4-7. Each description of it is in the arena of interpersonal relationships. We would expect from the larger context that Paul might want to instruct us on how to prophesy in love, how to exercise faith in love, and how to give sacrificially in love, but he does not do that. Instead he talks about exercising patience and being kind to one another. He talks about love eliminating envy and boasting, rudeness and selfishness; He says that love is not easily angered and keeps no record of wrongs. Paul has thus passed from the subject of gifts to the subject of relationships.

What is Paul saying to us through this subtle change in subject matter? Just this: Love must permeate and govern every aspect of our lives. Love is not to be exercised only in the use of our gifts and in the performance of our various Christian duties. Love is to be exercised in the home or at the office or in the classroom where our gifts are not a particular consideration. Love is to be exercised all the time in the most mundane duties of life, not just when we are engaged in Christian work. On the other hand, the absence of love in the ordinary duties and relationships of life can undermine and destroy the effective use of our gifts.

RECOGNIZING YOUR GIFTS

As we truly commit ourselves to do God's will, we may be sure He will so direct the course of our lives that we will begin to exercise our spiritual gifts and fulfill our function in the body of Christ. Throughout the course of time, however, it is important for us to periodically evaluate how God has directed our lives in service to others in the body. If we are to develop our gifts, we must know what they are.

Paul urged us to assess our gifts in Romans 12:3 when he said, "By the grace given me I say to everyone of you: Do not think of yourself more highly than you ought, but rather think of yourself with sober judgment, in accordance with the measure of faith God has given you." The context of this passage indicates that this is a call to serious assessment of our spiritual gifts. How, then, should we evaluate God's leading in our lives and recognize the gifts He has given to us for the good of the body?

Although no pat formula can be given, there are several suggestions that may be helpful in assessing our gifts. First, we must be sure we are committed to doing the will of God that He has ordained for us. It's been said 90 percent of finding God's will lies in our willingness to do it. Since God's will for us is consistent with His gifts to us, we may also say a commitment to *do* whatever God wants us to do is necessary in determining what our gifts are. Note, however, this willingness is a willingness to do God's will and a willingness to fulfill our function in the body. It is not a willingness to find out something about ourselves—that is, to find out what our gifts are. Rather, it is a willingness to do whatever God has appointed us to do in the body of Christ.

Assuming you have already committed yourself to doing the will of God, consider then how He has providentially led you. What has He given you to do, and, of equal importance, what has He *not* given you to do? What service in the body have you tried in which you have experienced His blessings on your efforts? What things have you tried in which you have not experienced His blessing? What opportunities to serve have been opened to you? What opportunities have in some way been closed to you?

Consider also your natural abilities and your temperament. While natural abilities are not the same as spiritual gifts, it is true spiritual gifts build on some of our abilities and temperament traits. For example, I consider myself to have the gift of teaching. The gift of teaching assumes, among other things, the ability to study and to organize the fruit of the study. I have always been a natural student, both by intellect and by temperament. I am much more comfortable with ideas and concepts than with tools and building materials. The gift of teaching builds on my natural ability and temperament.

One word of caution is needed at this point: Natural abilities and temperaments are not always a sure indicator of gifts. Many natural abilities in music and various creative skills have been buried out on a mission field because the person was called by God to a pioneer missionary endeavor. Our abilities and even our temperaments have to be laid at the foot of the Cross and left there for God to either take up and use in our lives or, if He so chooses, to leave lying at the foot of the Cross.

Perhaps the most crucial and telling criterion for assessing your gift is the confirmation from other Christians. The exercising of your spiritual gift should result in ministry and blessing to others. They can tell if you have ministered to them. If you have, they will let you know, either by words of appreciation and encouragement or by requests for you to minister to them again. Finally, you might seek confirmation of what you believe your gifts to be from Christians you respect, people who know you well enough to help you in your evaluation.

Whatever your gifts are, you may be sure that when you exercise them you will find joy and fulfillment as you share with others in the body the gifts God has given you.

CHAPTER 14

WORSHIPING GOD

WHAT WILL WE be doing in eternity? We won't be evangelizing, because we will only be in the company of the redeemed. We won't be discipling because all the redeemed will have been conformed perfectly to the likeness of Christ. In fact, every Christian activity in this life will be completed except for one. That one exception is *worship*. As you read the book of Revelation and see the various scenes in heaven, one thing is apparent. Worship is going on continually. So if we want to grow up into spiritual maturity, we need to learn to worship in this life. We must learn to do imperfectly now what we will be doing perfectly for all eternity.

What is worship? In Scripture the word *worship* is used to denote both an overall way of life and a specific activity. When the prophet Jonah said, "I am a Hebrew and I worship the LORD, the God of heaven, who made the sea and the land" (Jonah 1:9), he was speaking of his whole manner of life. In contrast, Psalm 100:2 says, "Worship the LORD with gladness; come before him with joyful songs." The psalmist there speaks of a specific activity of praising God. This is the sense in which we normally use the word *worship* today.

These two concepts of worship—a broad one and a narrower, specific one—correspond to the two ways by which we glorify God. We glorify God by ascribing to Him the honor and adoration due Him—the narrow concept of worship. We also glorify God by reflecting His glory to others—the broader, way-of-life manner of worship.

========

WORSHIP AS A WAY OF LIFE

Look at how this broader concept is taught in a familiar verse from Paul: "Therefore, I urge you, brothers, in view of God's mercy, to offer your bodies as living sacrifices, holy and pleasing to God—this is your spiritual act of worship" (Romans 12:1). To offer our bodies as living sacrifices is to worship God. That Paul intended not just the physical body, but one's entire being, is implied from Romans 6:13, where he speaks of offering ourselves to God and the parts of our bodies to Him as instruments of righteousness.

To offer your body to God necessarily involves offering your mind, emotions, and will to Him also. It is the wholehearted dedication to God of heart, mind, will, words, and deeds—in fact all that you are, have, and do. It is a total way of life. Paul called that our spiritual act of worship.

To attempt to worship God in only the narrow sense of praising Him without seeking to worship Him in our whole way of life is hypocrisy. Jesus rebuked the Pharisees because they were going through outward motions of worship, but their hearts were not committed to God. "You hypocrites!" He said. "Isaiah was right when he prophesied about you: 'These people honor me with their lips, but their hearts are far from me. They worship me in vain; their teachings are but rules taught by men'" (Matthew 15:7-9).

I cannot judge the hearts of people, but it seems our Christian community today is full of people who appear to worship God on Sunday but live for themselves the rest of the week. I'm not suggesting they are living a lifestyle of gross sin. On the contrary, most of them live highly respectable lives; otherwise they wouldn't be in church on Sunday morning. But they do not live to the glory of God during the week. They live for the fulfillment of themselves and their goals.

Since all that we've covered in this book up to now speaks to worship as a way of life, from here on in this chapter we'll focus on the more limited definition of worship. But it's important to understand that a lifestyle of worship is the necessary foundation for all our praise and adoration, both privately and corporately.

WORSHIP AS PRAISE AND ADORATION

What really is this worship in the sense of praise and adoration? The Puritan Stephen Charnock called it "nothing else but a rendering to God the *honor* that is due him."[1] John MacArthur defined it as "*honor* and *adoration* directed to God."[2] A. W. Tozer gave a more expanded meaning. He said that God "wants to cultivate within us the *adoration* and *admiration* of which He is worthy. He wants us to be *astonished* at the inconceivable elevation and magnitude and splendor of Almighty God!"[3] Note the words I emphasized in these quotations: *honor*, *adoration*, *admiration*, and *astonishment*.

One of the best biblical descriptions of worship is Psalm 29:1-2:

> Ascribe to the LORD, O mighty ones,
> ascribe to the LORD glory and strength.
> Ascribe to the LORD the glory due his name;
> worship the LORD in the splendor of his holiness.

This is the essence of worship: *Ascribe to the Lord the glory due His name.* Before we can do that, however, we have to understand something of the glory that is *due* Him. We have to begin grasping His greatness, sovereignty, holiness, wisdom, and love. We have to meditate on and pray over Scriptures such as Isaiah 6:1-8, Isaiah 40, Daniel 4:34-35, Psalm 104, and 1 John 4:8-10 that teach us about these attributes.

In the Daniel passage, notice how Nebuchadnezzar worshiped God after his seven years of animal-like insanity:

> At the end of that time, I, Nebuchadnezzar, raised
> my eyes toward heaven, and my sanity was restored.
> Then I praised the Most High; I honored and glorified
> him who lives forever.
>
> His dominion is an eternal dominion;
> his kingdom endures from generation to generation.
> All the peoples of the earth are regarded as nothing.
> He does as he pleases with the powers of heaven
> and the peoples of the earth.
> No one can hold back his hand or say to him:
> "What have you done?" (Daniel 4:34-35)

Nebuchadnezzar praised and honored and glorified God. He acknowledged the eternalness of His person, His dominion or rulership, and His absolute sovereignty. He then goes on in verse 37 to exalt God's righteousness and justice:

> Now I, Nebuchadnezzar, praise and exalt and glorify
> the King of heaven, because everything he does is
> right and all his ways are just. And those who walk in
> pride he is able to humble.

Nebuchadnezzar didn't quibble with God over the severe chastening he had received at God's hand. Rather he praised God's justice. He knew he had received what he justly deserved. At the same time we can reasonably infer that he praised God for His mercy, which he had experienced in being restored to his kingdom and very likely in being brought into a genuine conversion encounter with the living God.

The lesson here is that in order to render heartfelt worship to God, we must be gripped in the depth of our being by His majesty, holiness, and love; otherwise our praise and adoration may be no more than empty words.

Isn't this one reason why much of our worship today is so anemic and heartless? We aren't likely to have the kind of encounter experienced by Nebuchadnezzar. But we can encounter God in His Word as we meditate on it and pray over it, asking the Holy Spirit to reveal to our hearts the glory of God as seen in His infinite attributes. We must do this if we're to worship God in a manner of which He is worthy.

HEARTFELT THANKSGIVING

It has been said that we praise God for who He *is* and thank Him for what He *does* for us. Such a precise distinction between praise and thanksgiving probably isn't wise, but the statement does call our attention to the fact that thanksgiving is an important aspect of worship.

In Romans 1:18, Paul speaks of "all the godlessness and wickedness of men," which has called forth God's wrath. Then he tells us how all this ungodliness and wickedness began: These people "neither glorified him as God *nor gave thanks to him*" (verse 21). Their wickedness was a result of their failure to worship God—their failure to give God the glory and thanksgiving due to Him.

Luke's account of ten lepers who cried out to Jesus to heal them is an insightful story that helps us see how important thanksgiving is to our worship. Jesus told them, "Go show yourselves to the priests." As they went on their way they were healed.

> One of them, when he saw he was healed, came back, praising God in a loud voice. He threw himself at Jesus' feet and thanked him—and he was a Samaritan.
> Jesus asked, "Were not all ten cleansed? Where are the other nine? Was no one found to return and give praise to God except this foreigner?" (Luke 17:15-18)

Ten were cleansed; only one returned to give thanks. Jesus emphasized the uncalled-for disparity between the many and the one: *Where were the other nine?* The lesson is obvious. God does note when we take time to thank Him and when we don't.

I believe God also takes note of the sincerity and depth of meaning we put into giving thanks to Him. The expression "Thank you" covers a vast range of situations, from the most ordinary spur-of-the-moment kind to those with eternal significance. I might say "Thank you" to a friend for lending me his pen for a moment. I use the same words to thank God for my salvation, which is of eternal consequence. How can I distinguish between these two infinitely different deeds of kindness when I must use the same words to express my thanks in both situations?

The answer lies in the depth of meaning we put into those words. To say with deep feeling to my friend who lends me his pen, "Thank you with all my heart" would be effusive and inappropriate. He would probably think I was a bit strange. But to say those words to God with deep feeling is not only appropriate but the very minimum we should do.

Being healed of leprosy—or of cancer in our time—lies in between the lending of a pen and the gift of eternal life. Obviously it is much more significant than borrowing a pen. At the same time it is vastly *less* significant than having eternal life. If we had to choose between being healed of cancer and receiving eternal life, the decision for any Christian would be easy. Yet how often do we express our thanksgiving to God for the gift of eternal life with as much depth as the one leper who "came back, praising God in a loud voice" and who "threw himself at Jesus' feet and thanked him"?

David also combined praise and thanksgiving in his beautiful prayer of worship as recorded in 1 Chronicles 29:10-14:

> David praised the LORD in the presence of the whole
> assembly, saying,
>> "Praise be to you, O LORD,
>> God of our father Israel,
>> from everlasting to everlasting.
>> Yours, O LORD, is the greatness and the power
>> and the glory and the majesty and the splendor,
>> for everything in heaven and earth is yours.
>> Yours, O LORD, is the kingdom;
>> you are exalted as head over all.
>> Wealth and honor come from you;
>> you are the ruler of all things.
>> In your hands are strength and power
>> to exalt and give strength to all.
>> Now, our God, we give you thanks,
>> and praise your glorious name.
>> "But who am I, and who are my people, that
> we should be able to give as generously as this?

Everything comes from you, and we have given you
only what comes from your hand."

David began by praising God for His surpassing glory. Note how he heaps up words of praise and adulation: *greatness, power, glory, majesty,* and *splendor*. David was not simply being eloquent. He was pouring forth heartfelt praise. He acknowledged here what we see in Psalm 24:1—everything in heaven and earth belongs to God. He recognized God's sovereignty: "You are exalted as head over all." And he confessed that all wealth and honor come from God. Then he thanked God for the ability to be so generous. In fact, he explicitly affirmed that everything he and his officials had given toward building the temple was only a returning to God what had first come from His hand.

It's difficult to separate thanksgiving from praise in our worship of God. A better practice is to join them, as we see in Psalm 100:4-5:

Enter his gates with thanksgiving
  and his courts with praise;
    give thanks to him and praise his name.
For the LORD is good and his love endures forever;
  his faithfulness continues through all generations.

———

PRIVATE WORSHIP

Both private and corporate worship—that which we do individually and that which we do with other believers—are taught in Scripture. For example, David says in Psalm 69:30, "I will praise God's name in song and glorify him with thanksgiving." Here David refers to his own personal worship.

If we aren't spending time daily worshiping God, we're not apt to contribute to the corporate experience of worship. If we aren't worshiping God during the week, how can we expect to genuinely participate in it on Sunday morning? We may indeed go through the motions and think we have worshiped, but how can we honor and adore One on Sunday whom we have not taken time to praise and give thanks to during the week?

In contrast to the once-a-week worshiper (and that term itself is an oxymoron), David worshiped God continually. "I will extol the LORD at *all* times," he said; "his praise will *always* be on my lips" (Psalm 34:1, emphasis added).

Again in Psalm 145:1-2 he told God,

> I will exalt you, my God the King;
>> I will praise your name for ever and ever.
> *Every day* I will praise you
>> and extol your name for ever and ever. (emphasis added)

He goes on to say, "Great is the LORD and most worthy of praise; his greatness no one can fathom" (verse 3). In these words we sense the depth of his feeling, an emotion that could not be "pumped up" with a once-a-week visit to the house of God.

===

ESSENTIALS OF WORSHIP

Jesus spelled out the first essential of worship when He said to the Samaritan woman, "God is spirit, and his worshipers must worship in spirit and truth" (John 4:24).

The "spirit" in which Jesus says we must worship God is the

human spirit. It is what Paul often refers to as the heart. Worship is not just an external act. True worship must come from the heart and reflect a sincere attitude and desire.

Jesus said we must also worship "in truth." Our worship must be in harmony with what God has revealed about Himself in His Word. It is possible to have zeal without knowledge (Romans 10:2). For example, if we stress only one side of God's attributes—say, His mercy and love—without also stressing His sovereignty and holiness, we're not worshiping in truth.

A second essential in worship is that we must always come to God through Christ. Paul is explicit about this: *"In him and through faith in him* we may approach God with freedom and confidence" (Ephesians 3:12, emphasis added); "For *through him* we both [Jews and Gentiles alike] have access to the Father by one Spirit" (Ephesians 2:18, emphasis added). And having come through Christ, we can approach God with confidence: "We have confidence to enter the Most Holy Place by the blood of Jesus" (Hebrews 10:19).

In the Old Testament era there were three restrictions on entering God's Most Holy Place in the temple: *Only* the high priest could enter, and *only* once a year, and *only* with the blood of atonement (see Hebrews 9:7). But now, says the writer to the Hebrews, all believers may enter. In fact, we have *confidence* to enter, implying free and continuous access.

So two restrictions have been removed, while one remains: *We still must come by the blood.* Only now it is not the blood of a goat but the blood of Jesus. Though we have been born again and though our sins—past, present, and future—have been forgiven, we must still approach God through the merit of Jesus Christ. We are never of ourselves worthy to come before a holy God.

Because of the continued presence of indwelling sin in our hearts and our consequent lack of perfect obedience, we are never, of ourselves, worthy to come into the presence of God and worship. We must always come through Christ. Our "spiritual sacrifices," as Peter said, are "acceptable to God *through Jesus Christ*" (1 Peter 2:5, emphasis added).

The writer of Hebrews taught this same truth: "*Through Jesus*, therefore, let us continually offer to God a sacrifice of praise—the fruit of lips that confess his name" (Hebrews 13:15, emphasis added). It is always through Jesus that we offer to God a sacrifice of praise. Our most fervent expressions of worship, either in prayer or song, are unacceptable to God if they are not offered through His Son.

A third essential to worship is a heart free from cherished sin. David said, "If I cherished sin in my heart, the Lord would not have listened" (Psalm 66:18). To cherish a sin is to hold on to some sinful disposition or course of action we know is wrong. Perhaps you have been wronged by someone and you know you should forgive as the Lord forgave you. Yet you are unwilling to let go of that unforgiving spirit. Instead you cherish it and nourish it. You cannot truly worship God when you are in that state.

Perhaps you are involved in some unethical business practice that may be barely legal but does not meet the test of love, of treating others as you would like to be treated. In your innermost heart you know the practice is wrong, but you're unwilling to give it up because of the financial cost. Or perhaps you love to gossip. The Holy Spirit has convicted you of it many times, but you enjoy it. You get a perverse delight out of running down other people because it makes you feel good about yourself. If you're resisting the convicting work of the Holy Spirit, you are cherishing sin in your heart, and you cannot truly worship God.

Let me emphasize that there's a difference between struggling with sin and cherishing it. You may genuinely desire to forgive another person. In your mind you have said many times, "I forgive her," yet your own corrupt heart keeps bringing it up. You cry out to God to change *you,* but for some reason He allows you to keep struggling. That is not cherishing sin; that is warring against it. What you need to do in that case is to appropriate the blood of Christ to cleanse your conscience so you may worship freely (see Hebrews 9:14).

HELP IN OUR WORSHIP

Perhaps the idea of private worship is new to you. You have always thought of worship as something to do on Sunday morning at church with other believers. Now you see the importance of private, daily worship, but you don't know how to begin.

Of course the first thing you have to do is select a time. I have my personal worship in conjunction with my "fellowship with the Father," which I have each day before breakfast. I consciously and deliberately enter His presence through the merit of Christ, acknowledging my sinfulness, pleading His cleansing blood, and confessing that only through Christ can I call God my Father.

The joy of realizing my sins are forgiven and I am accepted by the Father through Christ lifts my soul to praise and thanksgiving. I often use a biblical prayer of praise such as David's in 1 Chronicles 29:10-14. I take time to thank God for my salvation and for the way He has led me in my Christian life throughout the years. I consider where I could have been had God not intervened in my life at various points.

I reflect on my humble beginnings as a child growing up during the depression years in a working class family and consider where God has brought me. I think of Jacob's words that describe so accurately my own life's story: "I am unworthy of all the kindness and faithfulness you have shown your servant. I had only my staff when I crossed this Jordan, but now I have become two groups" (Genesis 32:10). I acknowledge my absolute dependence on God for life and daily provision. I thank Him for a godly wife and for children who follow Him.

As I read the Bible, I often come across passages of Scripture that remind me of some truth about God, or perhaps even reveal to me something new. When that happens I pause once again and worship.

Submission to God is also an important part of worship. After the death of my first wife, a friend passed on to me a little saying by an unknown author that helps me express my submission to God:

> Lord, I am willing
> To receive what You give;
> To lack what You withhold;
> To relinquish what You take;
> To suffer what You inflict;
> To be what You require.

I keep a copy of this in my prayer notebook and pray over it several times a week. I've also added another sentence: "And to do what You send me to do."

Our posture in worship is also important. Old Testament passages that speak of worship often speak of bowing down. For example, Psalm 95:6 says, "Come, let us bow down in worship, let us kneel before the LORD our Maker" (see also Deuteronomy 8:19; 2 Chronicles 20:18 and 29:30; Job 1:20; Daniel 3:5; Ephesians 3:14; Revelation 22:8). Kneeling or bowing down is a physical expression of reverence and submission. I don't want to imply that you must always bow down to worship effectively, though I think we should do it frequently. The important thing is your attitude of heart.

WORSHIP IN HEAVEN

I began this chapter by observing that worship will be our principal activity in heaven. I can think of no better way to end this chapter and this book than to look at two of these examples found in the book of Revelation. Read them slowly, carefully, and prayerfully, asking God to create in you the same excitement about worship that there is in heaven.

> Each of the four living creatures had six wings and was covered with eyes all around, even under his wings. Day and night they never stop saying:
>
> Holy, holy, holy
> is the Lord God Almighty,
> who was, and is, and is to come.
>
> Whenever the living creatures give glory, honor and thanks to him who sits on the throne and who lives for ever and ever, the twenty-four elders fall down before him who sits on the throne, and worship him who lives for ever and ever. They lay their crowns before the throne and say:
>
> You are worthy, our Lord and God,
> to receive glory and honor and power,
> for you created all things,
> and by your will they were created
> and have their being. (Revelation 4:8-11)

Then I looked and heard the voice of many angels,
numbering thousands upon thousands, and ten thousand times ten thousand. They encircled the throne
and the living creatures and the elders. In a loud
voice they sang:
    "Worthy is the Lamb, who was slain,
    to receive power and wealth and wisdom and
strength and honor and glory and praise!"
    Then I heard every creature in heaven and on
earth and under the earth and on the sea, and all that
is in them, singing:
    "To him who sits on the throne and to the Lamb
    be praise and honor and glory and power, for ever
    and ever!"
    The four living creatures said, "Amen," and the
elders fell down and worshiped. (Revelation 5:11-14)

Do these examples reflect your own heart? If so, thank God that
worship is already part of your Christian walk. If not, prayerfully go
back over the essentials of worship I've set forth in this chapter, asking
God to help you make them a central part of your life. Then you will
begin to grow in worship.

======

As we come to a close, let me remind you of what I call the "bookends"
holding up all the truths in the Christian life. I urge you to place your
trust daily in, first, the righteousness of Christ by which the infinitely
holy God accepts us with joy and, second, the power of Christ that

enables us to live the Christian life confidently as we grow toward maturity. These truths bracket and hold together our entire Christian experience. Of course, the image of bookends has the usual limits of a metaphor, because bookends are inanimate objects. Remember that the righteousness and power of Christ are marvelous, living truths. They are the continual gift of a living Person, the Lamb of God who alone is worthy of our perpetual worship.

NOTES

CHAPTER 1

1. Archibald Alexander, *Thoughts on Religious Experience* (Edinburgh, Scotland: The Banner of Truth Trust, 1967), p. 165.

CHAPTER 2

1. This, of course, does not mean God is indifferent to our sin. But even in dealing with our sin, God always acts out of His love for us.

2. Martyn Lloyd-Jones, *Romans: An Exposition of Chapter 6, The New Man* (London: The Banner of Truth Trust, 1972), p. 8.

3. Stephen Brown, "The Song of Grace" (Part I), 1 Peter 5:6-14, cassette recorded message (Key Biscayne, Fla.: Key Life Tapes, 1990).

4. Ernest F. Kevan, *The Grace of Law* (Grand Rapids, Mich.: Baker Books, 1976), p. 63.

5. Charles Hodge, *An Exposition of the Second Epistle to the Corinthians* (London: The Banner of Truth Trust, 1959), p. 133.

6. Philip E. Hughes, *The New International Commentary on the New Testament, Paul's Second Epistle to the Corinthians* (Grand Rapids, Mich.: Wm. B. Eerdmans Publishing, 1962), p. 258.

CHAPTER 3

1. John Calvin, *Calvin's New Testament Commentaries, vol. 10, The Second Epistle of Paul to the Corinthians, and the Epistles to Timothy, Titus and Philemon*, ed. David W. Torrance and Thomas F. Torrance, trans. T. A. Smail (Grand Rapids, Mich.: Eerdmans, 1964), p. 371.

CHAPTER 4

1. I have used the *English Standard Version* (ESV) for 2 Corinthians 3:18 because it, as well as most other versions, says "beholding" the glory of the Lord, whereas the NIV says, "reflect" the Lord's glory. Although both meanings are feasible, I believe the context favors the use of "beholding."

2. William S. Plumer, *The Grace of Christ, or Sinners Saved by Unmerited Kindness* (Keyser, W.V.: Odom Publications, n.d.; originally published 1853), p. 278, emphasis in original.

3. Plumer, p. 279.

4. John Murray, *Redemption—Accomplished and Applied* (London: The Banner of Truth Trust, 1961; originally published 1955), pp. 144–145.

5. Murray, p. 145.

6. Murray, p. 146.

7. Murray, p. 147.

CHAPTER 5

1. The Navigators has emphasized Scripture memorization for over sixty years. Their *Topical Memory System*, which teaches principles of memorization and provides sixty key verses of Scripture to memorize, is available from NavPress and may be purchased through your local Christian bookstore. If you have never developed the discipline of Scripture memorization, I highly recommend this program.

CHAPTER 8

1. J. I. Packer, *God's Words* (InterVarsity Press: Downers Grove, Ill., 1981), p. 193.

2. Packer, p. 200.

3. Packer, p. 193.

CHAPTER 9

1. James Fraser, *A Treatise on Sanctification* (Audubon, N.J.: Old Paths Publications, 1922; originally published 1774, revised 1897), pp. 464–465.

2. For the original quote, see John Brown, *Analytical Exposition of Paul the Apostle to the Romans* (Grand Rapids, Mich.: Baker, 1857, reprinted 1981), p. 93.

3. William Romaine, *The Life, Walk and Triumph of Faith* (Cambridge, England: James Clarke & Co., Ltd., 1793, 1970 edition), p. 280.

4. George Smeaton, *The Doctrine of the Holy Spirit* (Edinburgh: The Banner of Truth Trust, 1882, 1958 edition), p. 228.

CHAPTER 13

1. Warren Myers, *Pray: How to Be Effective in Prayer* (Colorado Springs, Colo.: NavPress, 1983), pp. xv-ii.

2. There seems to be disagreement among Bible scholars on whether a person may have more than one gift. I personally believe in the affirmative, but the issue is not crucial to this discussion. In the text, I use gift or gifts without any particular significance between singular or plural.

3. I am indebted to J. D. Jones (1865–1942) for this illustration taken, though not quoted verbatim, from his book *An Exposition of First Corinthians 13*, originally published in 1925 by Hodder & Stoughton of London and republished in 1982 by Klock & Klock Christian Publishers, Inc., Minneapolis.

CHAPTER 14

1. Stephen Charnock, *The Existence and Attributes of God* (1853, reprint, Grand Rapids, Mich.: Baker, 1979), 1:212.

2. John MacArthur, *The Ultimate Priority* (Chicago: Moody, 1983), p. 14.

3. A. W. Tozer, *Whatever Happened to Worship?* (Camp Hill, Penn.: Christian Publications, 1985), p. 26.

ABOUT THE AUTHOR

JERRY BRIDGES is a staff member of The Navigators Collegiate Ministries where he is involved in staff training and also serves as a resource person to those ministering on university campuses.

He has been on the staff of The Navigators since 1955. From 1979 through 1994, he served as Vice President for Corporate Affairs. In addition to his work in the Collegiate Ministries, he also serves from time to time as a guest lecturer at several seminaries and speaks at numerous conferences and retreats, both in the U.S. and overseas.

Jerry is the author of several books. His most well known is *The Pursuit of Holiness*, which has sold more than a million copies. Other titles include *The Practice of Godliness*, *Trusting God Even When Life Hurts*, *Transforming Grace*, *The Discipline of Grace*, *The Gospel for Real Life*, *The Crisis of Caring*, and *The Joy of Fearing God*.

Jerry and his wife Jane live in Colorado Springs, Colorado. They have two adult children and five grandchildren.

Four more extraordinary books by beloved teacher Jerry Bridges.

The Pursuit of Holiness
Twenty-five years ago, this book opened Christians' eyes to a new way of "running the race." Today it still inspires a real and tangible holiness.

978-1-57683-932-4

The Gospel for Real Life
The gospel provides for our eternal salvation, but how does it benefit us day to day? Find out how the gospel sets you free from sin's defeat and daily transforms you into Christlikeness.

978-1-57683-507-4

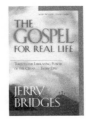

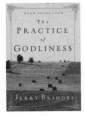

The Practice of Godliness
It's easy to get caught up in doing things for God instead of being with God. Learn how to be godly in the midst of life by being committed to God rather than activities.

978-0-89109-941-3

The Discipline of Grace
Jerry Bridges offers a clear and thorough explanation of the gospel and what it means to the believer.

978-1-57683-989-8

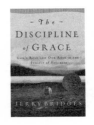

To order copies, call NavPress at 1-800-366-7788
or log on to www.navpress.com.

NAVPRESS

Discipleship Inside Out™